ONE MAN's BATTLE AS A BLACK CONSERVATIVE

WHY I COULDN'T
STAY
SILENT

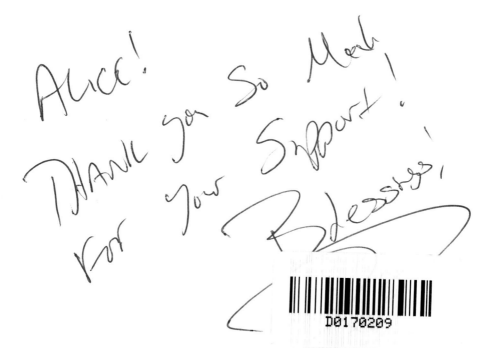

DAVID J. HARRIS JR.

TABLE OF CONTENTS

DEDICATION

"This book is dedicated to… My mother, for her passion and commitment to life. You always encouraged me to be the best version of myself, to think for myself, to put God first, family first, and never settle for less than what I believed God had put in my heart… I can't wait 'til I get to see you again. Say hi to Papa and my Big Brother for me…

My father, for his tireless commitment to being a provider and for showing me what a hard-working and loyal family man looks like. Your commitment to family is amazing pops. Thank you for all that you've done for me…

Most importantly, I dedicate this to my bride. For I would not be the man that I am today if it had not been for her love, support, grace and commitment to seeing me become what she believed I could become. Jennifer, you never gave up on me. You always believed in me and I am so thankful that Papa handcrafted you just for me… You still to this day, amaze and inspire me…

And I dedicate this book to my daughters, Corbin and Skyler. I hope that you will always go after everything that's in your heart

7

and I pray that you will always keep God at the forefront of your dreams. I thank you both so much for all of the love and support that you've given me. You are the two most amazing gifts that God has blessed my life with..."

FOREWORD
BY CANDACE OWENS

"The world is on the brink of a major shift.

What may be perceived as political tension, bubbling beneath the surface of two ideologically disparate groups — is actually something far greater, far more deep-rooted, and much more likely to change the trajectory of the world as we know it.

It is a shift toward individual freedom.

Within America, our culture has suffered from a collectivist approach to thinking. Ideas, which were once sprung from critical assessment are now being manufactured on the basis of race, sex, and gender.

There is no group that has suffered the consequences of such collectivist associations more than the black community.

Our fidelity to the Democrat party, coupled with our false hope that government can facilitate solutions, has led to the overall collapse of our families, neighborhoods, and incidentally, our futures.

But the tides are shifting. People are beginning to question political orthodoxy and new leaders are emerging to help steer open minds into the unchartered possibilities of their futures.

One such a leader is David J Harris Jr.

I was first introduced to David in a true millennial setting: Facebook. Scrolling through my comments section, a follower of my mine suggested that I look into him and included a link to one of his videos.

I am so grateful that I obliged and clicked that link.

Along with many other black conservatives, I have openly surmised that the biggest problem facing the black community is not the exaggerated topics of racism or police brutality—it is father absence. It is the disappearance of strong male role models from both the household and from within the community, that has led to a deterioration of our prospects.

David represents an example of just such a strong role model that I wish only to multiply, and amplify.

You have already purchased this book and are therefore well on your way to learning much more about his personal convictions than I could ever detail to you in an opening.

I wish to instead inform you of his character beyond these pages:

David is a man driven by intense passion, strong intellect, and endless positivity. His dedication to providing a focused, honest, and inspiring message of hope is something that I believe will reverberate—beyond this book and in chorus with the millions of hearts and minds that are on the brink of a shifting paradigm."

CANDACE OWENS
Director of Communications
Turning Point USA

INTRODUCTION

L et me start off by just telling you a little bit about myself. I was not raised in a very political household. I don't remember my parents being very active towards any particular political candidate while I was growing up. I don't ever remember my parents wanting to go to rallies for candidates. I really don't even remember my parents watching speeches of candidates on the news. I do seem to remember sometimes my parents would listen to the president speak, but probably only because it was plastered all over every channel on the TV, dominating the airwaves for a presidential address.

My dad was a very hard-working individual. He was a large (for that time) black man, standing about 6' 3", weighing probably 260 lbs, and his weight wasn't from fat. He had a full-time job, and worked hard to make sure that we had a roof over our heads, food on the table, and clothes on our back.

Back then, my mom was a petite, reddish blonde. She was a fiery and to-the-point woman. She held a sales job at a car dealership for a while when I was young, and broke every state record standing at the time. (Again, this was at a time when a woman selling cars was abnormal.)

My parents wanted me to get good grades. They felt that education was important, but I don't remember them checking my work too much unless it was time for my report card. They would see my A's and my B's and say, "Well, you probably could have done better to get those B's up, but a good job overall.

My adolescence was pretty void of politics. It was more a time in which our Sundays were encumbered with church, family get-togethers and the big events of the rest of the year seemed to be more focused on us moving from place to place as my parents tried to provide my sister and I with a better home. We started out in a mobile home and eventually made our way up to a three story home in Klamath Falls, Oregon. Then, my parents got divorced. I was nine. During the custody battle I remember the judge called me into his chambers, and asked me who I wanted to live with. I remember telling him that I wanted to live with my dad, thinking that he looked more like me. Even at nine years old I was trying to figure out where I fit in. What my identity was … I may have to tell the story of how that decision truly shaped the rest of my life, but not in this book. So I went to live with my dad, and we moved to Redding, CA.

Life, as I remember it, was just... life. It consisted of schoolwork and hanging out with friends after school. I tried not to get on my dad's bad side by leaving a mess around the house or talking back, which I often liked to do. I remember he used to always say, "You talk way too fast, slow down!" (That's something I still try to remember to this day)

My teenage years were probably filled like most young boy's, minus the cultural differences of having a mother that is white and a father that's black. Living with one parent through the school year, and the other (my mom) during the summer breaks. At school, I tried really hard to just fit in, sometimes to my own detriment. I'd often talk way too much, too long, or would laugh too loud at a joke that wasn't that funny. Yeah, I was "that" kid... I battled immense insecurity over my parents' divorce, and over the fact that I was a biracial kid in a predominantly white town.

I'll share in this book how some of those instances of racism not only came at me from the white community, but also from the black community.

I shared how un-political we were growing up to set a tone for the fact that I never dreamed of writing a book that covered politics. I shared how mixed up I was as a kid to again, relate that I never dreamed I would write a book about issues of race. I ultimately want to let you know that although I do tackle some tough issues in this book, my goal in sharing this information with you, is to allow you insight into the circumstances that caused this seemingly un-political individual to become very outspoken on issues of politics, race, and social issues.

I will also cover topics about my faith, and why "abortion" is more than just a word to me. I understand that not all of you are going to share the same faith, but I hope that by me revealing to you a little about *why* I believe the way I do, you may come away with a better understanding for those people called Christians. I understand that not all Christians are the same. On the contrary, that would be like saying, "blacks are the same or all whites to the same".

All I can do is offer my own understanding of what the core values are for my beliefs, and hope that you can gain an appreciation of that in the process. I can honestly tell you that 20 years ago, 10 years ago, even a year ago, I did not think I'd be writing a book about the content that you're about to read, but based on the heightened emotional climate that is constantly swirling around all of us on a daily basis, I feel that it is important... as an American, as a member of the black community, and most importantly, as a member of the human race.

I want to thank you for reading my first book, and I'd like to challenge you with a question... While reading this, ask yourself, where am I wrong...? I have no doubt that this book will either resonate with you, or draw fire from an opposing side… kind of like who I am, and what I'm made up of. I am a creation of what was once two opposing sides. I have a great understanding for both the black and the white side of my family. Each side operates, dances, sings, cooks, and in most ways behaves differently than the other side of my family, and I somehow, am stuck in the middle.

Although for decades I did in fact feels stuck in the middle, I now believe I understand why I'm here. I hope that from reading these pages, you will be inspired to use your voice in whatever capacity you have, with whatever imagination you have, to spread truth, light, hope, and love… for there are far too few of us doing this these days. But I, for one, cannot stay silent any longer.

one

WHY I COULDN'T STAY SILENT

I had been watching the campaign for Donald Trump and Hillary Clinton very closely like I had never watched a campaign before. There was so much turmoil and negative rhetoric that I saw between these two candidates that were running to become the next commander-in-chief of our great nation, and I continued to see what I believed was a negative spin on all of the things that Donald Trump said during different points of his campaign. I witnessed how CNN would take small clips of sentences spoken by Donald Trump, that when taken out of context, made him seem cruel, and even racist. Then they would run with only a clip of his speech, and push it all over social media and the news. Why would they do this? Did they want to create a narrative that Donald Trump was a racist, a sexist, a bigot and not worthy of being the next POTUS?

I remember an instance in which I was discussing Donald Trump with a seemingly politically-neutral individual, and he brought up the very quote that CNN had run with that I knew to be false. He said, "Donald Trump is a racist! He hates Mexicans, and said that they are all rapists and murderers! Who would say that, unless he was a racist?"

15

The problem was, I had actually seen Trump speaking at the rally from which that quote had been taken. I asked him if he'd seen the entire speech. He said no, that he had seen it on CNN, and heard Trump say it with his own mouth. I tried to share with him that that quote was taken out of context, but he didn't want to hear it. He had his mind made up. The amount of hatred and animosity that I had encountered with people towards Trump during the election was shocking to me.

But what shocked me the most, as a Christian, and as a lover of humankind, was when I Heard Hillary Clinton from her own two lips share that she believed not just in abortion, but in partial-birth abortion, and that the unborn baby should have no rights to life whatsoever.

During the third debate between Trump and Hillary, this was what stood out to me the most. Hillary shared that she believed it was ultimately the right of the woman carrying the child to choose whether or not the unborn baby should be allowed into this earth. I had previously heard her share that even if the baby inside the mother's womb was nine months in the making, until that baby came out of the womb, she believed that the baby did not have any rights to life. During the debate, I heard Donald Trump adamantly share his position for rights to life for unborn babies, to such a degree that he actually had said on several occasions he believed that a woman choosing to end the life of an unborn baby should be held liable, and even face prosecution.

I heard a clear difference in the direction that each of these two candidates wanted to take our country. I saw a chasm between life and death, and ultimately what I believed would be the ultimate demise of our country. If we allowed our country to move in a direction that allowed women to kill their unborn babies at will with no regards to the life of that innocent baby, we would be heading down a road from which there would be no return. Partial-birth abortion is horrific. It is inhumane. It is literally torture to that unborn baby. To speak about something as heinous as partial-birth abortion - the way that the baby is dismembered piece by piece – and for the next POTUS to even consider that as an option for ending a human life, there was no way I could stay silent any longer. I hopped on my Facebook page and went live to share my thoughts with the couple thousand friends that I had in hopes that someone, anyone, would see what I saw, and share my views with others.

Here's the transcript from that video:

"I cannot keep silent any more. I just watched the debate, and I gotta tell you, as a Christian, a Black man - and that's the order - it's God first for me. It's God first for me, period. As a Christian and a Black man, I one hundred percent support Donald Trump for President of the United States. The fact that he brought up so many points that Hillary dodged over and over again is alarming. She's good. She's a career politician. But the one thing that he brought up in the very beginning, in the very beginning, he brought this up, the issue on abortion. And that's what stands out to me the most.

I just listened to an abortion doctor that shared how he had performed over a thousand abortions, and he spoke about what happens during a partial-birth abortion ...the fact that babies are dismembered before they're pulled out of their mother's body... I felt my heart fall into my stomach. And Trump, as he spoke about abortion, you could hear, and you could feel the passion in his voice when he was talking about that...

It has to stop. We as Americans, if we want the blessing, if we want God's blessing on us as a country, it absolutely has to stop!

That's the clear division... period. That's the absolute clearest division that I see between Hillary and Trump. I absolutely believe in so many other things that he's said and done as far as what he'll do for people, what he'll do for

Black America, Black youth, and Latino youth.

Hillary and the Democratic Party has said it over and over and over again. They talk, and then they do nothing. They do nothing except they expect my Black brothers and sisters to vote Democrat, yet they do nothing for the Black communities, the Latino communities, and they never have. He said that, and he nailed it. "They want your vote and they come back four years later and they say, give us your vote again." Why do we believe that we have to vote Democrat?

There is ignorance that has been instilled like slavery on the black man and woman that think that they have to vote Democrat because that's how it's always been. That is BS! And for me and my house, we will serve God first. We will serve the Lord first. I believe in the Bible first, and then it's my ethnicity, and that's not even what it's about. You know what? I bleed red just like you do. I love my black brothers and sisters, just like I love my white brothers and sisters. You know why? Because even though ever since I was a little kid, I dealt with racism, even though my mother is of Irish descent. I've dealt with racism my whole life, but I've never been looked at as white kid. I've been looked at as black, a light skinned, Black African American man.

I've dealt with racism, but you know what? God kept my heart soft. He kept my heart gentle. I'm thankful for that. It was God that did that in me, and the loving people around me that kept me that way. But I am a Christian first. I am a Bible-believing individual first.

Now Trump nailed so many topics that she had nothing to say to debate him. She had nothing to say. The Wikileaks, the things that she said that were leaked in her emails. The exposing of the Democrat Party specifically causing chaos at Trump rallies. What is that about? Are You Kidding Me?? And that should be on the news everywhere. Yeah. She had nothing to say about that. She had nowhere to go. It wasn't even just about those issues. It wasn't the failed foreign policies that, yes, she's been in charge of foreign policies for close to a decade now, and it's a mess!

All of those things combined, plus me being a businessman. Yes, I am a businessman. This is my company (pointing to the logo on my shirt that reads Uncorked Health and Wellness) I love the opportunity to help people live healthier and more fulfilled lives. I've been a business owner for 20 years, over half my life. I absolutely believe in a businessman's ability to help our economy over a politician.

She wants to say, "Oh, Trump, he got a forty million dollar loan and that's why he's successful". He admitted he got a one million dollar loan. If I could get a million dollar loan to start a company and turn it into a ten-plus billion dollar juggernaut, I'd say that speaks volumes! That speaks pretty stinking loud to the average American.

That's what this country needs. But beyond that, beyond that, the sanctity of marriage, you know, I have nothing against somebody that chooses an alternative lifestyle. I love all people. And we all have issues or beliefs that others may not agree with. Some people's issues are exposed, some are hidden, but if we know that we have issues, and we go to God with those issues, and we ask him for help with those things, then he will help us.

God loves every single person. The shortest and complete definition of God in the Bible, is "God is Love"... He loved me when I was doing some really bad things. I have not always been the man I am today. It's been God's love, and grace, and his favor and mercy on me that's gotten me to where I am, but people never gave up on me. I don't give up on anybody, and I don't judge or condemn anyone. But God's Bible does say there's certain things we just should not do. Now, I absolutely believe that we need to stop killing unborn babies. Period! Hillary is for this. She wants to extend it, and here's the problem. When you extend it, it will get abused. They will abuse abortion when it's more liberal, when they say up until the baby is born it has no rights. And we cannot let that happen. That is wrong, and she said it. She said they have no rights up until they're born. If for no other reason than that, we cannot let that woman be in charge of our country. We cannot let that woman be in charge of our country! They will abuse it, and you will see more and more that it will become normal, or who-knows-what will happen to this country when they are killing babies and selling baby parts. Planned Parenthood got caught in the act, and on video, saying that they sell baby parts! And she wants to continue to fund them. Is that not ok to anyone else? Shouldn't that wake everyone up?

Is that not a warning to every person that's been born? You were once a baby in the womb. You were once inside the womb, and now you're out here, alive, living... and want to say "Screw the unborn! They're in the womb, they have no rights!" That's exactly what you're saying if you support Hillary, period!

If for no other reason than that clear distinction, and the fact that the next president will elect Supreme Court justices that will either push the abortion law further down the road than where it is right now, making it more and more legal and liberal for women to kill unborn babies, or we put someone on the Supreme Court that says it has to stop. We have enough blood on our hands. If that's the only reason, that's enough. If that was the only reason, that is enough … because it has to stop.

I posted something earlier, somebody said "you can't trust Trump, he's a this, or he's done that". He's at least apologized. A lot of the crap that they're saying about him has been debunked. Hillary has yet to apologize for anything that her husband has done or that she's done to the women that Bill has been accused of abusing. She has yet to apologize. She won't even address it. Does that not ring alarming to anybody? Yet she wants to talk about women's rights.

It's up to us. The American people. It's up to you. It's up to me. We have to get these clear choices out there. It's a clear separation. It's a very clear separation from what we have, and where we want to go as a country, because the Supreme Court justices that are picked are going to choose the direction of this country for most likely the next 25 to 40 years.

I have two daughters that are 18 and 20 years old. They will be well into their late forties, or even fifties, and have to deal with the justices that are nominated by the next president. They'll have kids. I'll have grandkids. What kind of country do we want to give our children's children? That's what a good leader thinks about. What do we want to leave for our children's children? That's the question. That's the only point. That should be the main point, and if that was the only point, then I would still vote for Trump, because that to me, is the cake. The icing is everything else that he wants to do. The cake is the fact that he wants to stop killing unborn babies, period. The icing is everything else that he wants to do for this country.

He doesn't want to take a salary. He doesn't need the money. He chose to step into the public limelight as a politician, to serve this country, and to be publicly put through a microscope and to have to deal with railing accusations getting thrown at him. He chose to do it to serve our country, and the fact that he wants to stop killing unborn babies should give him your vote. It gives him my vote! But besides that, he's also a man that I believe is seeking God. He's surrounding himself with Godly counsel. He's inviting men and women, filled with the Holy Spirit, to come in and give him counsel, which is something completely different than someone that just identifies as a Christian.

I had a talk with a gentleman today in the mall. He said he was a Christian. I asked him, "Do you ever talk to Holy Spirit? Do you know who that is?" The look on his face suggested that talking to Holy Spirit was totally foreign to him. I said, "You can talk to Holy Spirit just like I'm talking to you and you're talking to me". And I said, "Say this: Holy Spirit, reveal yourself to me. Reveal the Father God to me." And he repeated it, but he barely stumbled through saying it. It seemed like it was actually hard for him to say those words. I said, "Say this: Holy Spirit, reveal Jesus to me." He said those things, and then he stopped because he could feel something happening. I asked him, "Do you feel something on you right now?" He said, "Yeah". I said, "That's Holy Spirit. He's as evident and as real as I am talking to you right now."

Trump is at least seeking counsel from men and women that are filled with Holy Spirit and that want to give him Godly counsel as he runs this country. That speaks volumes to me as a believer. I don't believe Hillary is open to God at all. There's nothing that she's done or said that shows me that she is even remotely interested in what our God of the Bible, (who I love to call Papa, because He is a good, good Father)... there's nothing that she has said or done that says that she's open to hearing or listening to anything God has to say. But what speaks the loudest to me is her policy on abortion. Let's call it what it is. It's killing unborn babies. It's killing, and even dismembering, human beings ...and the most innocent among us... unable to fight for themselves. What kind of evil, wicked person wants to set that as a rule of law for our people, our families and our country?

We must stop her. We absolutely must! I hope you will. You obviously know who I'm voting for, and who I'm praying will win this election. I was praying for Trump the whole way through the entire debate. I was praying for him. He needs our prayers. Pray for him and share this. If this message meant something to you, share this, because I just could not keep quiet tonight. I had to jump on here. I had to. I had to share my heart. Thank you guys for watching and hearing my heart tonight. Trump 2016. We're praying for him. God bless you guys. We'll talk to you again soon."

I poured my heart out on that video. I had posted other live videos before and the most views I think one had ever gotten up to that point was a few thousand. Well the views on this video began to grow into the thousands that night. I couldn't believe it! The next day it was over 20,000 and 30,000 views. The next day, it was over 50,000 views and it continuing to climb. I was excited for the messages that I began receiving from people... Black, White, Hispanic, Asian... men and women alike... were all sending me messages, sharing with me how my video had inspired them, how it clarified to them what was most important in this race. Hundreds of the messages that people shared with me had a similar thread... that their entire family were Democrats... that they had been raised as a Democrat... that they had voted Democrat their entire lives, and that for them to vote for Donald Trump would mean going against their entire family. Some even feared of being ostracized from their family. But they shared with me that regardless of the backlash, after hearing my message they understood that they had to vote for life, and voting for life meant voting for Donald Trump!

The video grew to over 400,000 views in a couple weeks. The messages continued to pour in hour by hour. My inbox was flooded, and I enjoyed trying to read and reply to every single one.

The majority of those messages were positive. Most of those messages were supportive, and came from individuals of different races, different nationalities and different backgrounds. But unfortunately, and mostly from blacks, I received a ton of messages that called me a sellout, or called me a traitor. Messages that came from Blacks and Hispanics would call me a nigger, a porch monkey, a house nigger, coon, and other derogatory terms that I will not share here. I believe that these messages were all proof that I was on the right track. I was ruffling the feathers of those that could not see the forest through the trees. I was ruffling the feathers of those that had pledged their blind allegiance to a party regardless of that party's stance on life. But from the positive and supportive messages, I knew that my heart was being heard.

From that day forth, I had a new mission. I decided to start a public figure page where I believed my thoughts could have more of a reach, and hopefully expand the opportunity to share more of my beliefs with the masses. So I launched the *David J Harris Jr* Public Figure page on Facebook and that page has now grown to over 470,000 followers, or rather people that I call like to call friends. The positive messages have continued to pour in, as well as the negative, hurtful, spiteful, and even racist messages as well. However, one thing I know for sure. The place that I had lived most of my life, that place of not being too political, not being too far "out there" with my political beliefs, and based on what I felt was on the line for our country, I knew that there was no way that I could stay silent any longer.

two

WHEN BARACK WAS ELECTED, I CRIED...

I still remember where I was, at a little pub on the beach in downtown Laguna Beach, Ca. As I watched the results of the 2008 elections come across the news, I was filled with anticipation, an, unsettled... anticipation of what I believed would be a mistake if we elected Barack Hussein Obama to be the next commander-in-chief of our great country.

Leading up to the election, my mother, a strong conservative Christian, shared with me that I needed to look at his policies. She said I needed to pay attention to how he's voted in the past, and that I needed to pay attention to what he really stood for. When he shared messages of hope and change, and said that he wanted to fundamentally transform the foundation of our country, I heard something quite different than most of my Black brothers and sisters heard. I heard something that didn't register well in my spirit. I heard something that I felt was foreign, and something that was not for America. I love the freedoms that we as a people get to enjoy. Those freedoms come from the Constitution of the United States. That is the foundation of our country.

I love the way we operate as a free market capitalist country. As a businessman, I have enjoyed the fruits of being able to take an idea and bring it to fruition as a business. It's a wonderful thing to witness that idea not only providing individuals a service and a solution to a problem, but also giving those that wanted to share in that vision the opportunity to provide a good living for their families.

I started my first business when I was 20 years old. It grew to a place where I employed over 50 people, and in its peak years generated over two million dollars per year in revenue. I enjoyed the relationships that were created from that company. I enjoyed the families that were helped with the technology that we represented. Someone told me early in life that one of the only ways to become financially independent was to be able to sign your own checks. While I understand that is an extremely simple-minded approach to wealth creation, something about that statement stuck with me. The ability to take an idea and create a business around it is the goal of capitalism. That's one of many reasons why I love America.

We are the greatest country on the planet, and the greatest country in the history of the world because of our ability to operate without the overriding scrutiny of the government hovering over every facet of our lives. That is our foundation. So, what did Obama mean when he said he wanted to fundamentally transform America? I was concerned…

As I sat in that pub enjoying a cold brew, listening to the news, and hearing how state after state after state had given their vote to Barack Hussein Obama, I felt a deeper and uneasy lump fill my stomach. I remember viewing policies and positions that he had taken on abortion, on partial-birth abortion, and I could not understand how an individual with such harsh determinations for the value of an unborn life could run on those stances and potentially win.

As I was sitting there listening to these commentators share that Barack Hussein was going to become the next president of United States, another thought occurred to me, a thought that I hadn't even contemplated up to that point. I hadn't been thinking about the fact that the United States had not elected a Black man or a woman as president of the United States as of yet. It hadn't occurred to me because I had not been thinking about Barack solely on the basis of the color of his skin. I was thinking about Barack based on the content of his character, and the actions of his previous policies and voting stances. When I did begin to think about Barack as a black man, it hit me... it hit me that he would become the first Black president of the United States.

As that began to settle deep down in my heart and my soul, I felt a strange dichotomy taking place. I felt a resolute sorrow inside of me that the first black man to be the president of the United States was going to be a man that I sincerely felt would not adequately represent the heart and soul of Black America. Yet at the same time, I felt a tinge of relief, and even excitement, that America had chosen to get behind a Black individual to become the commander-in-chief. As I felt these two starkly different contrasting thoughts swirling around in my mind, I cried.

I cried because I did not believe that Barack Hussein Obama had the best interests of America in mind. I cried because I felt that while America had championed and rallied together to support a black individual as president - as monumental and historic as that was - I cried that it was going to be Barack Hussein Obama. Let's take a look at the legacy he left behind.

OBAMA'S ACTIONS

The Federal Reserve reported that 2007-2011, Americans lost 40% of their wealth. That was the greatest fall of wealth since the Great Depression. Some may attribute this to the crash of 2008, and suggest it was all Bush's fault. Let's look at some overall facts. George Bush's largest annual deficit was $500 billion. Obama's lowest annual deficit was $1 trillion. So yes, Bush was a big spender, but Obama was an even bigger spender.

One of his first acts as President was to return a bust of Winston Churchill, which was a gift from the British. Winston Churchill led the British during World War Two, helping us fight to defeat the Nazis. Why would he make it a point to get rid of a treasured piece of art depicting a man that was instrumental in helping us win the Second World War... especially right after stepping into the Oval Office?

I believe Obama disliked the fact that Churchill was a champion of colonialism, and that Churchill had ordered a strike on the anti-colonial uprising in Kenya. Obama's father and grandfather were both detained during this siege, so I believe it was personal. A blog put out by the White House disputed that Churchill's bust had ever been taken out of the Oval Office. This was later determined to be damage control, as they wound up apologizing for the blog's inaccuracy.

He was the first president to back Argentina, not Great Britain, in the dispute over the Falcon Islands. This may not seem like a big deal to most, but the fact remains that the United States had been on the side of our ally, Great Britain, during this dispute. Both Republican and Democrat presidents had supported Great Britain in the past, and Obama defected from this position.

Obama blocked the completion of the Keystone Pipeline, a project that would have created tens of thousands of jobs for Americans. He blocked offshore well drilling in America, but then gave billions of taxpayer dollars to Brazil, Colombia and Mexico to drill for oil off of their shores.[1]

Obama increased NASA's budget, but then lowered their horizon from trying to achieve a trip back to the moon, to reconciling with Muslims. Yes! He actually wanted this! Listen to what NASA Administrator Charles Bolden said in an interview in 2010 on the Al-Jazeera Network, a network that has been accused of having very anti-Semitic, and anti-American bias in the channel's news content.

"My first question to you is, why are you here in the region?" "Oh, I appreciate you asking the question. I'm here in the region as it's sort of the first anniversary of President Barack Obama's visit to Cairo, and of his speech where he gave what has now become known as an Obama's Cairo initiative where he announced that he really wanted this to be a new beginning of the relationship between the United States and the Muslim world. When I became the NASA administrator, or before I became the NASA Administrator, he charged me with three things. One was he wanted me to help re-inspire children to want to get into science and math. He wanted me to expand our international relationships. And third, and perhaps foremost, he wanted me to find a way to reach out to the Muslim world and engage much more with dominantly Muslim nations to help them feel good about their historic contribution to science, math and engineering."[2]

Are You Kidding Me? He wanted our country's administrator of NASA to reach out to the Muslim world to help them feel good about their historic contribution to science, engineering and math? I thought NASA was created as a civilian agency responsible for coordinating America's activities in space. Why in the world would we want our space program directors reaching out to the Muslim world to help them feel better?

Have we also forgotten that NASA was created in response to the Soviet Union's October 4, 1957 launch of its first satellite, *Sputnik I*? The *Sputnik* launch caught Americans by surprise, and sparked fears that the Soviets might also be capable of sending missiles with nuclear weapons from Europe to America. The United States prided itself on being at the forefront of technology, and, embarrassed, immediately began developing a response, signaling the start of the U.S.-Soviet space race. NASA was never created to be used as a political pawn to encourage other countries in their space efforts. It was created to help keep Americans safe and at the forefront of space technologies that would make sure we weren't caught by surprise by another country again.[3]

He supported the removal of Hosni Mubarak, an American ally in Egypt that worked to bring democracy to the region, but he did not support the democracy protests in Iran. Why would a President that is the leader of the greatest constitutional republic in the world, a country that prides itself in a proper democracy, want the removal of a leader that was trying to achieve the same thing in a predominantly Muslim region? His removal helped the Muslim Brotherhood grow stronger in Egypt.

Obama refused to take action to stop Iran from making nuclear weapons. He actually signed one of the worst deals with Iran that America has ever penned. It granted Iran billions of U.S. taxpayer dollars. Videos of Iranian leaders chanting "death to America" are continually being shared all over social media, yet Obama was caught sending billions of dollars in cash to Iran, on pallets, in the middle of the night! That sounds like something a mob boss would do!

Meanwhile, he slashed America's nuclear budget and planned further reductions, leaving us vulnerable to other nations in the world. When Obama became president, the U.S. had about 5,000 nuclear warheads. After the New Start Treaty, he planned to bring us down to 1,500. Then he asked the Pentagon to study how to bring our U.S. nuclear warhead arsenal down to 300!

Here's a message from Obama on nuclear power:

> "No single nation should pick and choose which nation holds nuclear weapons, and that's why I strongly reaffirmed America's commitment to seek a world in which no nations hold nuclear weapons."

A nuclear-free world? Are you kidding me??? The problem with that idea is that none of our enemies would commit to reduce their stockpile of nuclear warheads. So while Obama called for a nuclear-free world (which sounded great), the only country where he was capable of reducing its nuclear weapons, was ours. So why would he seek to do this? Well, if he wanted to level the nuclear playing field between America and every other dominant country in the world, i.e. Russia, China, and North Korea, this would do it. As Dinesh D'Souza puts it in his movie **Obama 2016**, this would be an anti-colonialist's dream. For them, it would be better to end American nuclear superiority and create a world where many countries have equal power. For some, it might very well turn out that they would have even more power than the United States.

What happens when other countries that would love to take control of our land see an opportunity to win a nuclear war in order to do so? Peace through strength has always been the American way.

Obama took the side of the Palestinians in the negotiations with Israel, even though Israel had been a long-standing ally of the United States, and even though most Jewish Democrats strongly supported Israel.[4]

All of these actions of Obama are a part of his legacy.

RACE RELATIONS IN AMERICA

My good friend Brandon Tatum, the Director of Urban Outreach for Turning Point USA, was formerly a police officer with the Phoenix police department. He was also on their SWAT team for a year and a half. He was a confessed Democrat, and was raised as a Democrat by his parents. He began to question the media and their narrative of Donald Trump, and decided to go to a Trump rally to see if there was any truth to the way the media had made Donald Trump and his supporters sound. What he experienced at that rally changed his life, and changed how he felt about Donald Trump and his supporters.

But it was when he heard Barack Obama standing at the White House, openly supporting Black Lives Matter and condemning the police, that he began to question the loyalties of our first black president. Obama condemned the supposed unwarranted assaults by the police against black individuals across the country. Obama's statements regarding the police were despicable. They incited a negative emotion inside of Black Americans across the nation to begin to believe that in some way white cops were just out to hurt or murder black individuals.

As a police officer, Brandon shared how on multiple occasions he had to put his life on the line and faced danger from criminals of all races. He shared how he's had to try to resuscitate individuals, and has even watched people die from a drug overdose, or from being shot. As an officer, hearing Barack Hussein suggest these things about police officers, he felt horrible. He felt betrayed by his own president - and a black president at that.

To think that a sitting U.S. president would take the side of what I personally believe is a racist organization that hides under a politically correct name, to support and endorse Black Lives Matter, is unthinkable. BLM has continued to incite violence and perpetuate a narrative that goes along with the mainstream media's message that racism in America has never been worse, promoting the belief that white cops are just out to do harm to black individuals, or are even out patrolling to kill blacks at will.

Our police officers have suffered the brunt of national attention being focused on them unrightfully. The national coverage of every shooting involving a white officer and a black suspect, had been plastered all over every TV station almost back-to-back across the nation. The media would continually fail to point out that in many of these instances, the individual that was killed was a criminal, was resisting arrest, or had a gun. Have there been individuals unlawfully killed by the police? Yes. But the numbers of individuals that have been unlawfully or suspiciously killed by the police are not solely comprised of the black community. In 2017, the number of whites killed by police was more than double that of blacks (not to leave out Hispanics, Asians and other races as well). So, there is *not* an all-out assault by racist cops towards blacks.

I love how Larry Elder responded to the claim that white cops were killing blacks at a rapid pace...

Dave Ruben of the Ruben Report was a confessed liberal before he got into this exchange with a man that knew the facts, and who based his summary on actual data, not emotional mainstream media rhetoric.

In an attempt make his point about racism in America, Dave used the narrative that the mainstream media had been purporting...

> Dave: "Cops are more willing to shoot if the perpetrator is black."

> Larry: "What's your data, and why? What's your basis for saying that?"

> Dave: "Well, look, I know a lot of people would say that."

> Larry: "Look, I know what they would say. I'm talking about what the facts are. The facts are that 965 people were shot by cops last year and killed. Four percent of them were white cops shooting unarmed blacks. And in Chicago in 2011, twenty-one people were shot and killed by cops. In 2015, there were seven. In Chicago, which is a third black, a third white, a third Hispanic, seventy percent of the homicides are Black on Black, about 40 per month, and almost 500 for the year last year in Chicago... and 75 percent of them are unsolved. Where's the Black Lives Matter protesters on that? The idea that a racist white cop is shooting unarmed Black people is a peril to Black people... it's BS, it's complete and total BS!"[5]

Wow! I couldn't have said it any better myself! It was from watching that exchange, and from seeing the directional change in party affiliation that Dave Ruben took, that I knew we could win this fight against the liberal mainstream media's narrative. It's also why we must always base our beliefs about social justice issues on facts.

In reality, that's how we should evaluate every aspect of what the mainstream media is telling us, or what our friends are telling us, or even what our own family may be telling us. We must base our stances on the issues on facts. When we do, if the individual to whom we are speaking, or if it's you, the one reading this right now... yes, you! If you are willing to admit that you don't know 100% of everything that there is to know, and because of that, there is always a possibility to make an adjustment to what you believe... We must be willing, if new information is given to support a different point of view, we must be willing to evaluate the merit of that information, and if it is indeed factual, we must be willing to change.

Larry continued his assault on the assumption of racism in America by delivering more facts.

> Larry: "And the reason for these so-called activists saying this is the assumption that racism remains a major problem in America. The media, CNN, especially MSNBC, runs down whenever a black cop shoots somebody, and there's some march on Washington. It's ridiculous. Half the homicides in this country are committed by, and against, black people. Last year there were 14,000 homicides. I'm not talking about suicides, I'm talking about homicides. Half of them were black, and 96 percent of them black-on-black. Where's the Black Lives Matter people on that?"

This is where Dave starts to understand the media's role in creating the biased narrative that he had been believing.

> Dave: "So that's where you would say that this is purely because of social justice, purely because they want ultimately for people to be angry enough to just keep voting Democrat?"

Larry: "That's right! And where is the evidence of a lack of social justice when a black suspect is killed by a cop? Believe me, the media is on it. People are watching it. And justice will, for the most part, occur. In Baltimore where Freddy Gray died in a van, you have a city that's 45 percent black, the City Council is 100 percent Democrat. The majority of the city council is black. The top cop at the time was black. The number two cop was black. The majority of the command staff is black. The mayor is black, the AG is black. Uhhh, and yet here we are talking about racism. I mean, it's, it's absurd."[6]

Watching the light bulb moments go off in Dave's mind when he was presented with facts was amazing. It was from that exchange of facts on an intellectual basis, not from an emotional rollercoaster, that a strong liberal changed his tune. He later admits that his conversion from liberal to the libertarian that no longer buys into the propagandist lies was because of that conversation he had with Larry, and proved to me that there is hope! Amazing!

In thinking about the Freddie Gray incident, there were riots in the streets in Baltimore. The tragedy was felt all across the country. The narrative that the mainstream media pushed on all of us caused friends and acquaintances alike to come up to me and apologize. Really? Are you kidding me??? Why are all these people apologizing to *me*? Were they apologizing because they felt that at some point in my life they were responsible for somehow causing racism to exist? Were they apologizing to me because I have dark skin, and suddenly because of having dark skin, I should watch out for the cops? It seemed so crazy to me...

So why would Obama purposely feed into and promote the same hate that all of the facts actually prove are wrong? And what about this... There was a study done by the University of Washington on police shootings. They discovered that cops were actually more reluctant, more hesitant to pull the trigger against a black suspect than a white suspect over the fear of being accused of racial profiling, as well as the fear that the civil rights establishment would come down on them. The conclusion was that whites are more likely to be shot by a cop under certain circumstances than a black person.

Over the last 30 to 40 years, the percentage of suspects killed by cops who were black has declined 75 percent, while the percentage of whites killed by cops has flatlined.[7] If anything, police are more concerned and afraid that they will be accused of being called a racist for shooting black people than for anything else. Obama had to know these statistics. He was the leader of the free world! Yet he stood there at the White House and publicly shamed the police, and embraced an organization that promotes a negative (and untrue) racist rhetoric.

If we look at almost every one of the incidents where a black man got shot and killed by the police, whether it's Eric Garner in New York (who died because he was selling drugs and resisted arrest), Tamir Rice in Cleveland (who was playing with a gun), or Michael Brown in Ferguson (who had just a committed a strong-arm robbery), almost every one of these incidents involved somebody resisting arrest.

three

POLICE AND RACISM

I can personally attest to the fact that all white cops are not just out looking for blacks to shoot. There have been three times in my life where I was apprehended by the police - even once at gunpoint - and I never got shot. When I was about 17 years old, I have to admit I was actually not a very good kid. I was involved in drugs and very heavily into the party scene. In this instance, I didn't have any drugs on me (thank God).

I was inside a local gas station getting some chips and paying for gas when a police officer walked up to me, called me by the name of "Red" and grabbed my arm, put it behind my back, and pushed me up against the wall.

He was very loud, and sternly (almost) yelling in my face. "What are you doing out, Red? What are you doing out? What are you into? I know you're into something illegal. What do you have going on?" All I could say to this officer was "I don't know who you're talking about, but my name is not Red." He continued to call me Red, and continued patting me down. I did not resist. I allowed him to pat me down, believing that when he realized that I was who I said I was, he would just leave me alone. Once he checked my ID, that's exactly what happened. He apologized, and he left me alone. He was white.

In 2011, I had just walked outside of a pub, and was about 30 feet away from the front door, giving directions to a friend that was coming to meet me. As I was standing there waiting, a police officer pulled up into an open parking space that was right in front of me, got out of his cruiser, walked right up to me, grabbed my hand and began to put it behind my back saying, "you're being detained". As he's grabbing my other hand, in which I'm still holding the phone and talking to my friend, I said, "I have to go. I'm being detained by the police." They cuffed me and said "Just stand there". I said, "I don't know what's going on officer. I just walked out of that pub. I don't know what you're looking for or who you think I am, but it's not me." The officer said, "just stand there and be quiet". I continued to plead my case and said, "Just go ask the bouncer at the pub. He just saw me walk out of it." The police officer continued, "Just stand there".

Bewildered, and a little embarrassed (I mean, who likes being handcuffed by the police on a busy downtown city street at night?), I stood there...not feeling very comfortable, not liking the position I was in, but not wanting to escalate the situation any further by being loud or obnoxious. What would that accomplish? I felt that if I just stood there long enough, eventually they would discover that I wasn't the person they were looking for, and that they would let me go.

After about seven or eight minutes, a police sergeant rolled up and walked up to me. I shared the same thing with him, saying, "Please go check with the bouncer. I just walked out of that pub. I have no idea what's going on." He continued to walk down the street to the bouncer to verify my story. He came back and ordered them to release me. He apologized for the mistake, and let me go. He, and the officer that had handcuffed me, were both white.

The officer shared with me that there was a robbery around the corner, and that a tall black man in a black leather jacket was the description given of the robber. Well, I am tall, and I was wearing a black jacket, so I guess I fit the description. So, feeling some vindication and justice, instead of getting all upset and calling the cops names or feeling like I was being racially profiled, I chose rather to understand their side of the story. They were looking for a criminal. They were looking for a criminal that fit my description. Had the criminal they'd been looking for been a white man in a white leather jacket, I'm pretty confident that they would not have rolled up and put me in handcuffs.

Believe it or not, about three weeks after that very incident, I was driving my car down a long stretch of rural road on the way to highway 99 in southern California. I was driving about 50 miles an hour, and I could see an old Ford or Chevy pickup truck about ten or so car lengths behind me. It was the kind of truck with the big back window that you could pretty much see through when looking at the truck in your rear view mirror.

I noticed a police car with his lights on coming up behind the truck that was behind me. I thought the truck was getting pulled over, and didn't think too much of it. Then I looked out of my window, and up in sky I noticed a helicopter with red and blue lights under it. Recognizing it as a police chopper, I thought, "Wow, they must really be looking for somebody." I looked in my rearview mirror again to see if that truck had gotten pulled over, only to see that the highway patrol car was actually right behind *me*! But - his lights were off. He was not trying to pass me, he was following about three car lengths behind me. As I looked for that helicopter again, it looked as though he was following along with my car! When I looked back in my rearview mirror, the police cruiser had turned his lights on with sirens blaring! They were pulling me over! I think I actually said out loud, "Wow this is crazy!" What in the world do they think I did?

I pulled my car off to the side of the road and waited for the officer to walk up to the car. I was smiling and couldn't wait for the officer to walk up to my car and hear that the music I was bumping was Christian hip hop. I was thinking it would be funny if they walked up and heard a "Praise the Lord" or a "hallelujah". After about 60 seconds of not having an officer walk up to my car, I turned my music down wondering what was taking so long. I put my head out the window to look behind me at the police car and what I saw was something no one ever wants to see. The police officer was out of his vehicle in a tactical position, crouched behind the open door of his cruiser with his gun drawn and aiming it straight at my head!

He was shouting, "Get your hands up, get your hands up." I have to admit, I still thought this was funny, but wasn't taking any chances with any sudden movements or loud outbursts. Up until this point, I don't think there was any way that they could have known that I was a black, and I had no idea why they were pulling me over. But I knew one thing... I was going to comply with every command! I could tell they meant business. So I put both of my hands up out of the window and said "My hands are up, my hands are up!" I kept both of my hands out the window fingers spread so they could see that my hands were empty. Two officers slowly made their way to my car with their guns still drawn, still pointed right at my head, and then asked me to get out of the car. I kept my hands up and was intent on not making any sudden moves. As the officer opened my door, I slowly got out of the car. They put my hands behind my back and patted me down. I literally had a smile on my face hoping that might lighten their mood. Whoever they were looking for was obviously in serious trouble, but I knew that it wasn't me. I said, "This is pretty crazy. I was just mistakenly identified as somebody else a few weeks ago and put in cuffs. Whoever it is you're looking for, it isn't me".

They searched my car, and asked if they could look in my trunk. While I know my rights and was aware that they couldn't look in my trunk without a warrant, I didn't feel this was the time or the place to slow down the impending revelation that I wasn't who they were looking for. They looked in my trunk, and finding nothing, lowered their weapons. The officer that had been holding my hands behind me, released them.

They then shared with me that there had been a home burglary in the area out of which I had just driven. The owners came home while the robbery was still in progress, and one of the robbers shot the homeowner, then fled the scene. The helicopter had been circling the area looking for what was reported as a light-colored sedan that had fled the area. Well, I had just left that area - and was driving a light colored sedan - a 1993 Lexus LS400, to be exact. So, the helicopter pilot thought that they had flushed me out of the area, and were sure that I was the criminal they were looking for. Being that the robber had shot and wounded someone, they were not taking any chances for what they believed was a potentially deadly threat.

The officers apologized for the misunderstanding and let me go on my way. I said to the officers, "No worries, I know you're just doing your job, and I'm thankful that you guys are out here serving and protecting the community". I felt good about my attitude. I felt good about the fact that I could reciprocate their actions with understanding and respect. Plus, it gave me one hell of a story to talk about, as I'm still sharing it today. It should be noted that all of the officers that I encountered that day... were white.

In another book, I might share how both of those instances of mistaken identity (which took place within three weeks of each other) were something that I absolutely believe God used to speak to me about choices I was contemplating in my life. Those events spoke loud and clear, and I felt confident in the decision that I was about to make.

Now, almost eight years later, based off of both of those instances, I can attest to the fact that I absolutely made the right decision. Actually, I made one of the best decisions that I've ever made in my life. And I feel as though Papa God used those insanely odd circumstances to speak to me.

After these encounters with the police, I can attest that if you treat officers with respect, and you obey their commands, I'm confident that you will make it out of any instance of being pulled over or having a gun drawn on you, alive… even if you're black.

I do not believe that white cops in America are just running around looking for a black guy to shoot, and I'm sure that there are millions of Black Americans that feel the same way. But for the Black Americans that may have bought into the same propaganda that Dave Ruben had, I believe that Obama's actions fueled and enhanced the negative race relations in our country. I'm so thankful for individuals that choose on a daily basis to put their lives on the line in service of their communities. I do not disregard the fact that I'm sure there are individuals that carry racism into their jobs in a variety of industries around the country, including the police department. There have been cases where cops were exposed for their racist slurs, and even ill intent, but those instances are far smaller and fewer than the media portrays. Those instances do not characterize all of the men and women that put their lives on the line and put those uniforms on every day across the country to try to help and save people's lives.

I firmly believe that racism in America took center stage because of Barack Obama. And, as unfortunate as it seems, I'd say that at least 98 percent… actually, I'll go ahead and say 100 percent… of the racism I have experienced over the last two years has been from my own Black community speaking out against me and my beliefs over who I support as the president of the United States.

So yes, when America elected our first Black man as the president of the United States, I cried… but it was not tears of joy. And now that Barack Hussein Obama is no longer in office, and more and more of his scandals have continued to come to light, I think all Americans, especially Black Americans, feel let down and even betrayed by who they thought they were electing as president. Since Barack continues to declare that he's a scandal-free president. I'm going to list 18 major scandals tied to his presidency.

four

THE SCANDAL FREE BARACK

L ove him or hate him, this is how America will remember him. These scandals that took place while he was our president can't be refuted. Yet he continues to say he was scandal free.

THE GREAT "STIMULUS" HEIST

Obama seems to think nobody will remember he grabbed almost a trillion dollars for "stimulus" spending, created virtually zero private-sector jobs with it, allowed a great deal of the money to vanish[8] into thin air, and spent the rest of his presidency complaining[9] that he needed hundreds of billions more to repair roads and bridges.

Vast sums of taxpayer money were wasted on foolish projects[10] that came close to the Keynesian economic satire of hiring some people to dig holes, and others to fill them in. Obama added insult to injury by appointing Vice President Joe Biden as the "sheriff"[11] who would supposedly find all that missing stimulus loot.

What Americans mostly ended up footing the bill for was an army of *government* jobs, and a lavish network of slush funds[12] for the Dem-

43

ocratic Party and its union allies. We're supposed to forget about all that, because years later, Obama's weak economy finally dragged itself to something like normal "official" employment levels... with the U.S. national debt *doubled,* and our workforce rate reduced[13] to Carter-era lows. Sorry, Democrats, but that's more than just failed policy. It's one of the worst government-spending scandals in our history. Democrats will howl to the moon over far, far smaller abuses of taxpayer money during the Trump administration, should any occur.

OPERATION FAST AND FURIOUS

Obama partisans seem to think any given example of abuse or inept-itude by their man stopped being a "scandal" the moment it seemed clear he wouldn't be impeached over it. Operation Fast and Furious, the Obama administration's insane program to use American gun deal-ers and straw purchasers to arm Mexican drug lords[14], is a scandal with a huge body count, prominently including Border Patrol Agent Bri-an Terry[15] and Immigration and Customs Enforcement Agent Jamie Zapata[16], plus hundreds of Mexican citizens. Agent Terry's family cer-tainly thinks[17] it qualifies as a scandal.

It is difficult to imagine any Republican administration surviving anything remotely close to Fast and Furious. The media would have dogged a Republican president without respite, especially when it be-came clear his Attorney General was putting political spin ahead of accountability and the safety of the American people. Remember, AG Eric Holder escaped perjury charges by claiming he didn't know what his own subordinates were doing – a pioneering, but sadly not unique, example of an Obama official using his or her incompetence as a de-fense.[18] For years afterward, we would hear some version of "I'm not a crook, I'm just completely inept" everywhere from the Department of Health and Human Services to the Department of Veterans Affairs.

But this was Barack Obama, so the media downplayed Fast and Fu-rious news... to the point where viewers of NBC News learned about the scandal[19] for the first time when Holder was on the verge of being held in contempt by Congress for it.

The relatively benign explanation for the astounding Fast and Furious scandal is that Obama's Justice Department wanted to release guns into the Mexican wild like so many radio-tagged antelope on a nature show, and follow them to arrest the big fish of organized crime. (In case you were wondering, no, the guns didn't *actually* have radio tags in them – that was tried in the much smaller, and utterly disastrous, Bush-era program[20] Obama's team used as a model for their vastly larger and *more careless* program.) This explanation becomes more difficult to believe the more you know about how careless the program was, and how abruptly it was shut down after Agent Terry's death.

The more sinister take on Fast and Furious is that the Obama administration wanted to create gun crimes in Mexico so they could complain about lax regulations on American gun sales – "for the purposes of creating a narrative that they could use in America to try and thwart our Second Amendment constitutional rights," as Andrew Breitbart put it[21] during a 2012 interview.

No matter which interpretation to which you subscribe, or how much you think Barack Obama knew about the program when he made scurrilous claims of executive privilege[22] to shut down investigations, it's an insult to a large number of murder victims to claim it wasn't a scandal. Unfortunately, the Bureau of Alcohol, Tobacco, Firearms, and Explosives hasn't learned as much[23] from the OFF debacle as we might have hoped.

Incidentally, the Border Patrol named a station in southern Arizona in Agent Brian Terry's honor. On New Year's Eve, persons unknown fired rifle shots[24] at a Border Patrol vehicle near the station.

ERIC HOLDER HELD IN CONTEMPT OF CONGRESS

This was a result of Operation Fast and Furious, but it merits distinction as a separate scandal in its own right. Holder was the first sitting member of a president's cabinet in the history of the United States to be held in contempt of Congress.[25]

Of course, Democrats closed ranks behind Holder, the White House protected him, and the media allowed Holder to spin the contempt vote as mere "political theater." In reality, it was a difficult step that responsible members of Congress didn't want to take, and it was fully justified by Holder's disgraceful conduct in the Fast and Furious investigation. No reasonable person could possibly review the way OFF was handled and conclude it was an example of transparency and accountability.

OBAMACARE

Everything about ObamaCare is a scandal, from the President's incessant lies about keeping your old plan if you liked it[26], to Rep. Nancy Pelosi's "we need to pass it to find out what's in it" dereliction of Congressional duty.

ObamaCare is a scam, pure and simple – sold on false pretenses by people who *knew* it wasn't going to work the way they promised. It doesn't feel right to dismiss it as a "failed" scheme when so much of the failure[27] was *intentional.* The bill was so sloppily crafted that Democrats were basically signing blank sheets of paper when they rushed it through Congress in a foul-smelling cloud of back-room deals. ObamaCare's designers precipitated a constitutional crisis by forgetting they left in a provision[28] to cut subsidies for states that didn't set up health-care exchanges – a provision that would have killed the entire program stone-dead two years ago, if it had been enforced as written.

The Supreme Court rewrote ObamaCare on the fly *twice* to keep it alive, which is a scandal in and of itself. President Obama delayed and rewrote the law[29] so often it was impossible to keep track of the changes, cutting Congress out of the loop completely. (Actually, someone *did* keep careful track of them[30], and the tally was up to 70 distinct changes by January 2016.)

That made some of Obama's rewritten mandates and deadlines blatantly illegal – but then, the Affordable Care Act isn't really a "law" in the sense American government understood the term. In practice it became something entirely new, an enabling act that gave the executive branch unlimited power to do whatever it thought necessary to keep the system running. If subverting the American system of government isn't a scandal, what is?

And let's not forget the scandal of ObamaCare's disastrous launch, foisted on the American people even though its designers *knew* it had severe flaws[31] – the billion-dollar website that cost another billion dollars to fix[32] after it crashed, accompanied by a constellation of state exchanges that blew up like Roman candles of bureaucratic incompetence. Let us not forget the absolute zero accountability for this disaster, mismanaged by everyone from President Obama to HHS Secretary Kathleen Sebelius, who treated the biggest new government program in several generations as though it were a minor side project that could be handled by subordinates with minimal supervision.

SPYING ON JOURNALISTS

Establishment media came about as close to falling out of love with Barack Obama as ever when his administration was caught spying on journalists.[33]

Why, if the reporter subjected to the most egregious surveillance, James Rosen, didn't work for Fox News, the mainstream media might have started treating Obama like a (shudder) *Republican.* Rosen was treated so badly that even Attorney General Eric Holder eventually admitted[34] feeling a bit of "remorse" about it. Apparently he felt so much anguish that he suffered temporary amnesia[35] and forgot to tell Congress that he signed off on the request to wiretap Rosen while he was testifying under oath.

THE IRS SCANDAL

The selective targeting[36] of conservative groups by a politicized Internal Revenue Service was a scandal grenade Democrats and their media pals somehow managed to smother, even though the story began with the IRS *admitting wrongdoing*.

Democrats suffocated the scandal by acting like clowns during congressional hearings, but at no point were the actual facts of the case truly obscured: yes, pro-life and Tea Party groups were deliberately targeted for extra scrutiny, their tax exemption applications outrageously delayed until after the 2012 election without actually being *refused*. If anything remotely comparable had been done to, say, environmentalist and minority activist groups by the IRS under a Republican administration, the results would have been apocalyptic.

There's also no question about the facts of the follow-up scandal, in which IRS officials brazenly lied[37] about having backups of relevant computer data. The American people were expected to believe that multiple state-of-the-art hard drives failed[39], and were instantly shredded instead of being subjected to data recovery procedures.

Luckily for the politicized IRS, the Justice Department was hyper-politicized under Obama too, so no charges were filed[40], and scandal kingpin Lois Lerner got to enjoy her taxpayer-funded retirement after taking the Fifth to thwart lawful congressional investigation.

BENGHAZI

This is the clearest example of Obama and his supporters thinking all of his pre-2012 scandals ceased to exist the moment he won re-election. Benghazi has been investigated extensively[41], and argued about passionately, since the night of September 11, 2012. Nothing can change the absolute fact that the Obama administration's story for the first few weeks after the attack was false, and they *knew* it was false. They spun a phony story to buy themselves a little time during a presidential election campaign, and it worked.

Nothing can change the fact that Libya was a disaster after Obama's unlawful military operation. Nothing can obscure the truth that Ambassador Christopher Stevens was sent into a known terrorist hot zone without a backup plan to ensure his safety. Everything else from Barack Obama, Hillary Clinton, and their defenders, is pure political spin. They dragged the story out for years, until they thought it couldn't hurt them anymore. That doesn't erase its status as a scandal.

HILLARY CLINTON'S SECRET SERVER

While we're on the subject of Hillary Clinton, her secret email server is an Obama scandal, too. She perpetrated her email offenses while working as his Secretary of State, and contrary to Obama's false assertions, he knew about it.[42]

Plenty of Obama officials other than Clinton played email games, most infamously EPA administrator Lisa Jackson, who created a false identity for herself[43] named "Richard Windsor" to get around government transparency rules.

THE PIGFORD SCANDAL

Named after a landmark lawsuit from the Bill Clinton era, the abuse of a program meant to compensate minority farmers for racial discrimination exploded under Obama. After years of left-wing attacks on Andrew Breitbart for daring to speak up about the scandal, the mainstream media – no less than the *New York Times* – finally admitted[44] his critique of the program was accurate in 2013.

Once again: if careless mishandling (or deliberate politicized misuse) of huge sums of taxpayer money isn't a scandal, what is?

NSA SPYING SCANDAL

Opinions about the nature and intensity of this scandal vary wildly across the political spectrum, but there's no doubt that Edward Snowden's pilfering of sensitive National Security Agency data was a debacle that damaged national security.[45] We had the ghastly spectacle of Attorney General Holder thanking Snowden for performing a public service[46] by exposing surveillance programs Holder's own administration didn't want to talk about.

President Obama and his administration made many false statements[47] as they tried to contain the political damage. The fallout included significant losses[48] for U.S. companies, and diplomatic problems[49] for the United States. Just about everything Obama did before, during, and after the Snowden saga damaged the relationship between American citizens and their government.

BOWE BERGDAHL

Bergdahl's ultimate fate rests in the hands of a military court[50] (unless Obama pardons him) but no verdict can erase the scandalous way[51] this administration conducted the prisoner swap that freed him from the Taliban and its allies. Many lies were told, the law was flouted, a deal of questionable wisdom was struck with his captors, and outraged Americans demanded recognition for the soldiers who died searching for Bergdahl[52] after he abandoned his post.

IRAN NUCLEAR DEAL AND RANSOM PAYMENT

Everything about Obama's dealings with Iran has been scandalous, beginning with his silence while the Green Revolution was brutally put down by the mullahs in 2009. The Iran nuclear deal was pushed with lies and media manipulation.[53] The infamous pallet of cash that wasn't a ransom[54] has become symbolic of Obama's mendacity and penchant for breaking the rules, when he thinks following them is too much trouble.

POLLUTING THE COLORADO RIVER

The Environmental Protection Agency managed to turn the Colorado River orange[55] under this greenest of green Presidents. Of *course* there was a cover-up.[56] Would you expect anything less from this "transparent" administration?

THE GSA SCANDAL

The General Services Administration was caught wasting ridiculous amounts of taxpayer money on lavish parties[57] and silly projects. Heroic efforts to resist accountability[58] were made, leaving puzzled observers to ask what it took to get fired from government employment under Barack Obama. (Alas, it was hardly the last time that question would be asked.) Oh, and *of course* there was a cover-up[59] from the Most Scandal-Free Administration Ever.

THE VA DEATH-LIST SCANDAL

The Department of Veterans Affairs has long been troubled, but the big scandals broke on Obama's watch, most infamously the secret death lists[60] veterans were put on while executives handed in phony status reports and signed themselves up for big bonuses. Obama was more interested in spinning the news and minimizing his political exposure than addressing problems; in few areas outside ObamaCare has his rhetoric been more hollow, his promises more meaningless.[61]

SOLYNDRA

The marquee green energy scandal wrote "crony capitalism"[62] into the American political lexicon, as corners were cut and protocols ignored to shovel billions of taxpayer dollars at companies with absurdly unrealistic business models. President Obama's ability to pick bad investments was remarkable. Luckily for him, American taxpayers covered his losses.

SECRET SERVICE GONE WILD

The Obama years saw one scandal after another hit the Secret Service, from agents going wild with hookers[63] in Columbia, to a fence jumper[64] penetrating the White House, and tipsy Secret Service officials driving their car into a security barrier.[65]

SHUTDOWN THEATER

Obama hit the American people hard[66] during the great government shutdown crisis of 2013, doing everything he could to make American citizens feel maximum pain – from using "Barry-cades" to keep war veterans away from their memorials[67], to releasing illegal alien criminals[68] from detention centers. It was an infuriating lesson for voters in how every dollar they get from government is a dollar that can be used against them, when they are impudent enough to demand spending restraint.

When you look a list like this, you have to wonder... why didn't the American people see all of these ACTUAL scandals filling the news networks the way we see the supposed Russian collusion scandal of Donald Trump?

five

DONALD TRUMP

I'd have to say that when I first heard that Donald Trump was going to run for president, I didn't really know what to think. I knew him as the billionaire business mogul that was on TV with his show, *"The Apprentice"*. I liked how he handled himself on the show, discussing how he would come to the conclusion on when to say to someone… "You're Fired". Obviously America did too, because it was a hit show, but it was still just TV.

I understood that he had built an international empire and had Trump hotels and properties all over the world, but I didn't know how he would handle running the greatest country in the world. So, like many of you that may have shared that sentiment with me, I began to do my research. I also began to watch him when he would speak at different events, talking about the issues on which he wanted to run, as well as the issues that he would tackle if he became the commander-in-chief. I heard him talk about ISIS. (At that time, terrorists' attacks were flooding the news.) It seemed like every time you turned on the TV, you'd hear about another ISIS attack, and more and more we began to hear of radical jihadist terrorists that were waging war, either here in our country or abroad, all in the name of their god.

Seeing all the information that continued to come out about these radical Islamic terrorists was troubling and disheartening, and it was most certainly frightening to think that they wanted to get into the United States. It didn't seem like our country was really doing anything to stop it. He was not afraid to call these Islamic extremists exactly what they are: Islamic extremists! Yet the mainstream media continued to cower when it came to identifying these terrorists for what they actually were, and they were afraid to specify the religion. I liked that about Trump. He didn't seem to care about political correctness. I liked the fact that when I heard him speak, he seemed to speak from the heart. He seemed to speak as we do. He seemed very passionate in his desire to see America be placed first in not only domestic issues, but in international issues as well.

I heard him speak about the issue of illegal immigrants flooding into our country, and identified the fact that there are some bad hombres that would love to get out of Mexico and come into the United States to rape or kill Americans. Instances of that nature had been all over the news as well.

Then I saw how the mainstream media began to slant things. I remember the first time I heard someone repeat the narrative that Donald Trump said all Mexicans were rapists and killers. I couldn't understand why they would say that, because I remember watching his speech, and where he spoke specifically about those that were coming in from Mexico. I very clearly remember him saying that it was not all of them, but that there are those kinds of criminals among them. They are coming across the border. They're bringing crime, they're bringing drugs, they're rapists, they're murderers, and I understood very clearly what he meant. I didn't believe he was calling all Mexicans rapists and murderers, yet that's what the mainstream media continued to tell Americans.

I didn't like the deceitfulness I saw taking place on the news about this man. I wondered why they were so slanted against him, and were trying so hard to make him out to be a monster. For years the media spoke about Trump was like he was a rock star. The media *loved* Trump before he ran for president. I remember seeing a clip of Trump when he was on the David Letterman show back in the 80's, and Letterman asked - almost *begged* - Trump to run for president. I remember seeing a video compilation of hip hop artists comprised of rappers of all colors that paid homage to Trump and were speaking about him almost reverently, because he embodied the American dream in their eyes. Rapper Ice Cube even concluded the same thing, saying "Donald Trump is what Americans love... Donald Trump is what Americans aspire to be... the American Dream". Even Oprah had Trump on her show in 1988, and asked him then if he would consider running for president! So, for the mainstream media and Hollywood icons to all of a sudden change their tune and say they would move out of the country if he was elected... was mind boggling to me...

I love that we now have a president who isn't afraid to open his mouth and say exactly what's on his mind. He isn't playing the politically-correct phrase game and isn't pandering to us, telling us what he thinks we all want to hear. Case in point (and something that led to one of my most watched videos after he was elected president) was when he spoke his mind about the NFL players kneeling.

When the NFL players started kneeling during the national anthem, I remember feeling absolutely disgusted at the disrespect that I felt was aimed towards our veterans and the American people. I was in disbelief that an NFL player would choose that moment in time, during a pastime that so many Americans cherish, that part before the game I consider to be the most sacred part of a football game, that the players chose right then to protest our flag and our anthem? Was disgusting to me. It's the time of a game where we get to take the opportunity to thank God for the freedoms that we have, and honor the Americans that have been willing to put their lives on the line for those freedoms.

I remember when I first saw my team take the field, where half of

them knelt during the national anthem. I felt so betrayed by the players
I loved. I felt such a betrayal by these individuals that get rewarded for
their athletic abilities to the tune of hundreds of thousands, or even
millions of dollars a year. They were using their clout to protest during
our national anthem, and supporting what I believed was a false narrative. The argument that "cops are killing blacks at an unprecedented rate had caused me to do my research. And the more I researched,
the more I discovered that cops killing blacks was not the real issue in
America. The largest issue facing the Black community was the fact that
90% of Blacks murdered in America were murdered *by other Blacks*.

It felt even worse to see these players taking a knee and disrespect-
ing our veterans, knowing that what they were protesting wasn't a real
issue at all. So now, in walks Donald Trump! While he was speaking
during a rally, he took some time to share his thoughts on the players kneeling in protest. Even though his choice of words may not have
been exactly right, I understood what he meant.

Sunday rolled around, and for this game I was at my friend's house
in Texas. My team's game was about to come on the TV, and I was a
bit nervous as to what I was about to see. As the game came on, and
the national anthem started, the camera panned to the side of the field
where my team was. When I saw over half of my team kneeling, my
heart sank. I couldn't watch any more. I no longer cared who won the
game. In fact, I hoped my team would lose!

I left the room, and walked out into the back yard to vent. I decided to go live on Facebook. Here is the transcript of the video. It was
watched over 15 million times. (edited just a bit for better reading:)

MY MESSAGE TO SUPERSTAR ATHLETES

"So let me get this straight. We have NFL players that are taking a knee
in protest. We've got the commissioner of the NFL that is basically sid-
ing with the players, saying that we need to be more understanding of

where they're coming from. We've got a Steph Curry that is refusing to go to the White House, basically voicing his opinion or his disapproval for President Trump. Something occurred to me, and I felt it was pretty massive, just a little while ago. Something pretty major occurred to me. First of all, you NFL players… you make millions of dollars every single year off of us, off of the American people, off of those that want to go to your games and support you, that cheer for you. We like to watch football and sports because it's a break from the rest of the world. It's a break from the rest of what's going on around us. We get to just get see some entertainment for a little while.

We get to enjoy something that we absolutely love, which is seeing our players perform at your peak from all of your hard work and talent. We appreciate what you have to put in to be able to perform at the level that you're at. We love to watch you, and share in your victories… so to turn on our television and the see you players taking a knee during the National Anthem is absolutely *not* what us Americans want to see!

Now something occurred to me… I'm going to share with you in just a second, and I hope that every single American shares this, because it doesn't matter what color you are, doesn't matter where you live in our country. It doesn't matter what team you like, if you're a USA-loving American, please hear this. Something massive occurred to me, but I'm going to take a minute to talk about the NFL players first.

You, million-dollar earners. You don't understand what it's like for us regular Americans. You do not understand what it's like for us that work our butts off every day. And a lot of us are working just to get by, just to pay our bills, just to be able to keep moving forward. You don't see things from our perspective. You live in a glass house, so to speak. You have big walls around your big gigantic houses, and then you want to take the opportunity during your work to protest? You're working! It's actually a fine for you to sit during the national anthem or do any kind of protesting during the anthem. You're out there to work, and you're out there to work for *us*. We're the ones that pay your bills. We're the ones that buy your jerseys. We're the ones that buy your tickets. We're the ones that turned the game on the TV to watch you play. We are the ones that are paying your checks! So, to then turn around and see you use your platform to disrespect our flag? Enough is enough! You do not get us! You don't get us...

Now this is for Steph Curry and Lebron James. You know what? You've been two of my heroes in the NFL and the NBA, and I believe to a lot of people also. Steph Curry, you're very open about your faith. You're open about your love for God. You're open about being a Christian and being a believer. You know what the Bible says? Pray for your president! It says, pray for those that are in rule over you. How come you're not doing that? How come you're choosing to use your voice and tell the world that you don't agree with our president and you're not going to go see him at the White House? And then you and all these other players want to get all up in arms because he rescinds your invitation? Are You Kidding Me???

You don't need to go see him. He doesn't need you to go see him. You get an opportunity to go see the president of the United States, and as a believer, you should want to go do that, and you refuse? So believers need to understand that we need to pray for those that are in power over us. It says that in the Bible, even if you're not a believer, you should appreciate the fact that we're supposed to pray for those that are in power over us. Here's the thing, Steph Curry, you don't get us either. Lebron James, you don't get the average American. You came right out of high school making millions of dollars. You don't get us, and yet you want to bash our president, and you want to use your platform to tell the world that you don't think that Donald Trump is fit to be president?

It's absolutely BS! You don't get us, the average American person. The people that voted for Donald Trump is the average American person that loves the United States of America and what this country was founded on. That loves what our military has done to give us the freedoms that we have. And you want to take your platform and use it as an opportunity to basically piss on it??

You know what, Donald Trump, he said it just a couple nights ago. I have a friend of mine, a Black American friend of mine and a pastor. He said, you know, he may have gone too far when he said, "sons of bitches". You know what? Maybe he should've said, "jackasses"! He wasn't talking about anybody's mother. He was just using the reference to exactly what those athletes are acting like. They're acting like a bunch of donkeys out there. Acting like a bunch of mules, a bunch of jackasses and donkeys. Mules are known for being stupid.

If you want to protest something, you should protest the Black-on-Black violence. That is, and always has been, a hundred times worse! If you look at the numbers, literally, if you look at the numbers, it's a hundred times more of a problem in the Black community. Black-on-Black crime rather than Police-on-Black crime. And I'm going to share another thing with you for those people that ever get pulled over by the police. I've been pulled over by the police. I've been a business owner since I was 20 years old. I have nice cars. I've been pulled over by the police at gunpoint. And guess what I did? I complied! The officer said "put your hands up!" and I did. I heard him saying, "Step out of the car". I said, "Yes, officer", and I stepped out of the car, and I kept my hands up. I complied! I'm not trying to get shot. I'm not trying to make a point. I'm not trying to take any built-up rage and animosity over what I think the police may be doing and then put that emotion into that situation! I had a police officer walk up to me on the street, thought I was somebody else, grabbed my hands and handcuffed behind my back and held me there, and I laughed the whole time. I didn't start acting a fool. I didn't start drama. I didn't resist. I just said, "It's okay. Soon enough, you'll know that I'm not the person who you're looking for". And it took about 8 minutes, and the police officer uncuffed me and he said, "Sorry sir, somebody in the area fit your description. We wanted to make sure it wasn't you"… and they let me go.

Ninety nine percent of the times a cop shoots a Black suspect, that suspect is resisting arrest, or even worse. Just like the video of that kid that got shot by the police, that the media blasted the policeman over the first video. Everyone on Facebook saw a partial video of this young guy that gets shot by the cop. Well, the media is trying to cause division. They're trying to stir things up. The full video was released by somebody else's camera, and it shows that that guy was going after the cop with a gun! He was trying to take him out!

Ninety-five percent of the shootings that have happened from police to Black or Hispanic, and I don't care what color they are... ninety-five percent of shootings would have been avoided had the person complied. It's "comply" not "resist". So if you NFL players want to get all upset about something, get upset and use your platform to tell the brothers and sisters out there of every color, tell your fans (and you have fans of every color). You have fans that cross the sex lines and race lines. Tell your fans to support our police, and if you get pulled over for something, comply. That's all you have to do. I saw the video where the where the gentleman is riding on a motorcycle and he's got a gun right in his back. He's a Black guy, and the police pull him over. They have him at gunpoint. He's got his hands up, and he just complied all the way until the police take away his gun. They check him out and they made sure he's safe, and then they let him go about his business. He didn't stir up a problem. He didn't start drama. If he had, he could be dead. We must use wisdom, people! We must use wisdom.

So please, for you believers that are out there in the sports world, read your Bible. READ it. It says, pray for those that are in power over you. Don't use your position to talk a bunch of crap about the police and the president and alienate half of your fans.

So, here's what hit me. Here's what hit me. Steph Curry, multimillionaire, Lebron James, multimillionaire, all these NFL players, multimillionaires. They don't get it. They don't get us, the American people. We had our voices heard when we voted Donald Trump into office. So here's what hit me...

We've got the media, we've got the NFL commissioner, we've got the NFL players, we've got NBA players on one side... and who do we have on the other side? US, We The People! We the American people are on the other side, and who's on that other side with us? Donald Trump. He is a person of the people, by the people, and for the people, and that should be the main topic, and that should be what we are all celebrating.

He is about the American people first, and he made that loud and clear when he went in front of the UN and told every other ruler of every other country, America comes first. And he said, you leaders of your own countries, you should be doing the same thing. You should be putting your country first, not Globalism. He put Americans first. He put Americans like you and me first. Let's pray for our president. Let's continue to believe for our president. But I think there's one more thing we all need to do. We all need to continue to vote. American people, we got out last November and we voted, and our voices were heard. Our man is in office. He's doing what he can to drain the swamp in Washington. Guess what? We must continue to do our part, and if that is turning off the TV when the game's on to make a point to these NFL players, these multimillion-dollar crybabies, then we need to turn the game off... because that's a vote too. When we're watching the games, we're voting as to where we're directing the money we send to our cable companies. They're tracking who's watching the games. Stop buying their jerseys. Don't go to the game. Don't buy tickets. Let it run out. Let's let the NBA and the NFL go. We the people come first, and we stand with our president. It's a battle between the haves and the have-nots. The multi-millionaires that have been living the dream have been in a bubble for decades... and us, the American people. We need to stand up and let our voices be heard."

That video resonated with You, the American people, and was viewed over 15 million times! It's because of the responses that I get from videos such as that one that I continue to share my views with the world.

So, does Trump say everything politically correct all the time? No. Do I care? No. I am happily enjoying seeing real issues that have continually gotten swept under the rug get brought front-and-center by his administration. While we are enjoying record low unemployment across all racial boundaries, seeing booms in the economy, taking our rightful place of leadership on trade in the world, and seeing a president that isn't afraid to say "Merry Christmas" and actually pray "in Jesus name"... I am most grateful that our commander-in-chief is placing the safety and security of his citizens above anything else.

six

RACISM IN AMERICA

As a young boy growing up, rather as a young multiracial boy growing up (I mean, if you looked at me, you wouldn't say, "oh, that's a white kid") I was considered light-skinned, with my little afro, and light chocolate complexion, with a big nose and big lips, traits that are normally associated with Black Americans. I've never been mistaken for anything other than Black, even though my bloodline has at least 8 other ethnicities as well.

I remember the first time I felt I had encountered racism. I was about 13 years old. I was at a water park in my hometown of Redding, California, which is about 97% Caucasian, and was standing in line to get on a waterslide. It was a crowded hot summer day, and there were tons of other people waiting in line to enjoy some summer fun.

I sneezed... and as my mom had taught me a good set of manners growing up, I said, "Excuse me". Standing right next to me in line was this tall white man that looked like he was in his late twenties or early thirties. He looked down at me and said, "There is no excuse for you..." and the look on his face was one of utter contempt. I didn't actually get it in that moment, even though that comment made me feel horrible inside. Later, I was thinking about it, and talking to a friend about what had happened, and my friend shared with me that the guy was probably a racist. Then it clicked. Wow! It made me feel even worse. To encounter pure hatred for no other reason other than the color of your skin has to be one of the *worst* feelings in the world.

For a person to openly degrade another individual without reservation, an individual that they don't know and have never met… is just tasteless, classless and evil. To have some preconceived idea about an individual by the way they looked? I didn't understand at the time that there were people in the world that wouldn't see you for who you are, but would see you for what they believed you are, based on some outward appearance and preconceived idea.

When I was about 15, I traveled to a city a few hours from my home town to stay with another family as part of our junior high school's dance competition. The competition was a two-day event, so we were invited to stay with local families of the dancers from the school at which the competition was to be held. I got to stay with Matt and his family. He was my age (about 15), and lived with his parents and his uncle. They had a nice home, a dog, and maybe even a white picket fence…   I made sure to always show respect and use those manners Mom had taught me. "Yes ma'am, no ma'am… yes sir, no sir…" You know, what used to be the normal way for kids to respond to adults. I enjoyed the time I got to spend with Matt, his family, and his uncle. I don't remember having too much of a dialogue with his uncle, but overall I felt that it was a very pleasant weekend.

A few weeks later, Matt reached out to share something with me. He started out with, "I hope you don't take this the wrong way". He shared how his uncle had been a racist, and had hated Black people for most of his adult life. He shared how his uncle had encountered a group of Black guys in college that roughed him up for no apparent reason, and it left a severely poor taste in his mouth about Blacks in general. He didn't expound on what else continued to sour his feelings towards Blacks, but he said that he'd carried that bitterness with him in his heart for years. Hearing that, I understood why Matt's uncle and I didn't have much dialogue that weekend... But then, Matt shared something amazing with me. He said that his uncle was shocked at how well behaved, and how well-mannered and polite I had been while at their home. He expressed to Matt his reasons for disliking Blacks and being bigoted towards them. Then he shared how after meeting me and watching my behavior, seeing a young Black man with manners, and respecting others, shattered the narrative that he had believed and held for years. It made him come to the conclusion that all Black people aren't alike! So, even though you may have met one bad apple in a bunch, that still doesn't speak for the bunch as a whole. That weekend that I spent with Matt and his family changed his uncle's life and his view of Blacks forever.

Discrimination comes in many forms. It can come in the form of a person being discriminated against racially, or because of their sex, because of the sexual orientation, because of their height, their weight, or any other outlying observation. Really, a person can be a bigot towards anyone else based on any external characteristic that triggers a response in the individual. More and more in today's society, I believe racism is evident far less in the form of color or gender, but rather in personal ideologies and beliefs.

I do, however, understand that racism in America has left a massive and negative stain on our country's history.

I'm not denying that Blacks in America went through tortuous and horrendous conditions in early American civilization. My great grandparents, and great, great grandparents lived through difficult and even atrocious conditions, all in the name of trying to live free. I do understand that there are bigoted and racist people that comprise a certain percentage of the population of our country, and that it may take decades, or even centuries, for that hate to completely dissolve. But, I also believe that what our ancestors went through and fought for in order for Blacks to be truly free in America, there's no way they would want any Black American to repay evil for evil, or discriminate against any group of people, based on the way things went down during those horrific past years.

I believe that the early Blacks in America were able to overcome the evil perpetrated against them largely (or at least in part) due to their faith in God. The Negro spirituals that so many of us know, and so many have forgotten or never even heard, share their deep belief and faith in a God that is good, and that will prevail, even in the face of evil. That faith is what I believe helped push Black Americans to continue to seek freedom, believing that it was ultimately God's will for Blacks to live a life of freedom. However, I feel that a large part of the Black community has left that simple faith in God and His love for all mankind and instead, has turned to a belief that says, "Because my ancestors were victims, I am a victim, and since I am a victim, I need to be rewarded or given a certain amount of privilege over another". This has spawned an outrageous belief on college and university campuses around the country that the white man now owes us, that whites are indebted to us. It has also triggered in the minds of some white Americans that the indebtedness is legitimate. This has created an illusion of White privilege and Black victimhood, when the fact is, millions of Americans are discriminated against every single day, regardless of race.

The Irish went through a discrimination period in the United States. The Italians went through a discrimination in the United States. The Japanese went through their internment and discrimination period in the United States. Yet I don't see these nationalities of people championing a voice that says, "I'm a victim, and you need to treat me and look at me as such". On the contrary, the Japanese have kept and stayed true to their humble belief in hard work and integrity, and are among the richest of Americans per capita in our country.

I feel if we could pull back the wool, the veil that covers all of this, behind the scene we would actually see an evil at work, an evil that seeks to divide people; An evil that seeks to divide a nation, an evil that seeks to pit man against man, brother against brother, and will use any means necessary to accomplish that goal. I believe that evil longs for the ultimate destruction of our country. That evil longs for the ultimate control of the world. It's an evil that's as old as time itself, and therefore I believe we cannot overcome evil with evil. We can only overcome evil with good, **Darkness cannot cast out darkness. Only light can do that. Hate cannot cast out hate. Only love can do that.** Thank you for your resolve, *Dr. Martin Luther King Jr.*, and for sharing those words with us. They still resonate this very hour, and are ever so needed at this moment in our country's history.

WHAT RACISM IN AMERICA USED TO LOOK LIKE

Racism in America used to look like actual clashes between the races. Obviously, the historical context of racism is indeed what the very definition of racism is, and is what was displayed. Racism was one person believing that another race is superior to another race, or one race of people is inferior to another. That is the classical definition of racism. We've had plenty of examples throughout history of different races, not just Black and White, but a variety of races clashing one against the other.

Let me talk to you about what racism is today. Today, racism takes on a different form. In today's racism, race is irrelevant. The color of your skin is irrelevant. Today, racism has taken on a form that is more adequately put as ideological racism, in which a person automatically deems another person as valuable, or less than valuable, based on their ideological beliefs. I think it'd be hard to find Blacks being racist against Blacks in the 1800's and early 1900's. Blacks stuck together. They felt that their family unit and their connection with their fellow dark-skinned brothers and sisters was a bond that surpassed any hate or division that would try to creep in. That bond was honored. That bond was respected, and believe it or not, that bond still exists today.

Often, when I see a Black man that I do not know (he can be a complete stranger to me), he will give me a head nod, and I will give him one in return. As small a gesture as it may be, raising his head up just a little bit says, "what's up, my brother"? It's a nod that connects us for who we have been, and what our ancestors went through. It's a bond that is very strong all throughout the Black community. So where has the breakdown occurred?

In gangs, if a Black American is wearing clothing that identifies them as being from a certain gang, Blacks from rival gangs will not give a head nod… Crips wearing blue, Bloods wearing red, and even if you are foreign to gangs or gang life, you'd better not find yourself in a Crip neighborhood wearing red.

A friend of mine (for the sake of privacy, I'll call him Michael) was driving through downtown Los Angeles several years ago with some friends when they found themselves in an unfamiliar neighborhood. They were lost. One of them was a very large man, about 350 pounds, and he happened to be wearing a red tee shirt. When they pulled off to the side of the road to ask for directions, they were immediately bombarded by Blacks that ran up to the car with guns drawn, shouting and calling him "Blood", and other explicit slurs. While Michael's friend tried to announce that he had nothing to do with Bloods, his pleas for mercy went unheard. The gang literally tried to pull him out of the car, and would have, if it were not for his enormous body. They ripped the shirt off of him in the process, and continued to scream at them, telling them they were lucky that they didn't kill them. Are You Kidding Me…? How in the world can such unfettered hate and unrestrained violence latch on to a community of individuals that used to have a mutual respect and love for one another?

It is victim mentality being displayed. To survive, a member must align with a band of brothers that they call family, and they rally around a certain color that represents their bond. I believe it is exactly the same type of gang-like behavior we see displayed over and over again in the media, but in the media's case, the color they support is political. Well-meaning Black Americans that identify as a Democrats go against well-meaning Black Americans that identify as Republicans. It's interesting to me that the desire to act confrontationally, yell, scream or defame another individual based on their political beliefs is mostly witnessed on the side of Black liberals against Black conservatives. I have yet to hear a story of a Black conservative that beat up, spit on, or screamed at a Black liberal just because of his or her political beliefs. So why has that type of hatred, and the violent tendencies that go with it, gotten such a stranglehold in the hearts of Black Democrats? Why isn't it displayed in the hearts and actions of Black conservatives?

In looking at the definition of the word conservative, you find these words: sober, cautious, and traditional. I think these are positive and timeless attributes when it comes to discussions, debates, conversations, or just plain living life. How many conversations have you had that didn't go so well because you weren't sober or cautious? So, as a lifestyle, especially in dealing with others of differing views, it would make sense that a conservative individual probably wouldn't go to the extremes that a liberal may go to.

When diving into the definition of liberal, aside from the political meaning of the word, liberal is more associated with "not being precise", or also "loose". We've all heard the saying, "loose lips sink..." (you know the word). Maybe it's even been our own loose lips that sank something at some point in our lives. Either way, being fast and loose isn't normally an easy path on which to grow stability. I know this is a simple overview of these two opposing views, but let's just keep it simple for a moment.

It could be said that a conservative is one that conserves, or tries to conserve, their emotions and their actions towards others, while a liberal seems to be more apt to loosely display their emotions. Therein lies a pair of dichotomies which an individual must understand exist, and then decide on which of those paths is their preferred way of life.

I do not believe we can create positive change in our communities while shouting, screaming, berating, bullying, or acting violently towards those that do not believe as we do. I believe if we're going to see positive change, we must start with open and honest dialogue, and come to the table with a soft heart and an open mind to truly look at the facts surrounding each issue. Facts are emotionless. There is no emotion in the fact that two plus two equals four. It just is. Regardless of how one thinks about the outcome of two plus two, they may hate the word four. They may have a deeply rooted bitterness towards the number four, but the emotion is irrelevant. It does not change the fact that four is the sum of two plus two.

With the understanding of facts being void of emotions, we as Americans, and especially the Black community, must desire to look at the facts in order to find the sum to make sure that our decisions are not based on emotion.

EMOTIONS

Emotions tend to change at the drop of a dime. A person may feel a certain way about their spouse one day, and then experience a heartache or an emotional letdown about a perceived outcome and feel as though they are not in love with their spouse a week later. However, marriage is a covenant. Marriage is a bond, and there's a reason why our vows say "'til death do us part". Marriage is a commitment, and it is a sum of the equation one plus one. I believe that the divorce rate would not be as high as it is if individuals looked at their marriage and chose to marry their partner based on a belief that marriage is a lifelong commitment and not a commitment based solely on emotions.

My wife and I have been married for 24 years. This coming April 2019, it will be 25 years. I can tell you that during our marriage there have been seasons of good, seasons of bad, and seasons of ugly.

There have been seasons of normalcy and laughs, good times, fun vacations and exhausting dance recital weekends with our girls… and seasons that were so stressful due to my work, or from working out of town, constantly battling depression, and drinking way too much to where my wife wanted to walk away. And there were times when she *did* walk away - and I had given her every reason to do so. Yet I believe it was because of her ultimate faith in God, and a commitment to her decision regarding the bond of marriage, that she chose to hold on to me and believe that I could ultimately become the man that she truly desired and believed I could become. I became that man when I chose to make a strong commitment towards sobriety. Alcohol had been ravaging my life, and my family had been caught in the crossfire too many times. I allowed my inability to control my drinking to dictate the outcome of my life. And too often, my wife was tired of believing that I would change. I'm glad that for our sake and our family's sake, she chose to hold on as long as she did… Now, as a man of sobriety, I am making decisions that my daughters, and my wife are consistently proud of…

Now that we've concluded that rabbit trail, let's get back to the topic of emotions. I think far too many of us base our beliefs on situations, or even our politics, based on emotions. Now some emotions are good to draw on, but only as long as the emotion is generated based on facts. Listening to some of today's leaders in the political arena, you can listen for a long time and not hear any facts. Worse yet, when they do spout off "supposed" facts, you have to look up the information to make sure they are telling the truth! I am very leery of an individual that speaks in such a way that incites emotions in the hearer without giving any facts.

RACISM IN AMERICA TODAY

Racism in America today exists between people of all backgrounds, nationalities, and cultures. Today, Black individuals don't look, sound, or talk alike. To feel, think or believe that they somehow should, is ridiculous. You can meet a black individual from the southern parts of Louisiana that may sound just like a white redneck from that same area. Yet those two could be best of friends. If that Black individual goes to Chicago or Los Angeles, as soon as he begins to talk (and based on how he looks), he will immediately be deemed as an outsider by other Blacks... even though he's black. Depending on who he interacts with, he may still even get that nod from a fellow black brother or sister.

Now it seems that what is at the forefront of racism in America amongst the Black community has solely to do with their political ideologies and beliefs. Let that same Black individual walk into Chicago wearing a Make America Great Again hat, he very well may immediately get verbally assaulted or berated because of that hat. This is exactly how gangs operate. How did we as the Black community ever allow it to get to this? How did we allow ourselves to take up the very same hate that the KKK held in their hearts? Why do we choose to carry that hatred and bitterness into the thoughts that we have about other individuals based on their political beliefs? Why can't we as Americans, regardless of race, choose to allow a person the freedom to speak his or her mind openly without fear of verbal bashing or being ridiculed? The hatred must stop. We as humans, as Americans, and especially those that call themselves Believers ... We... all of us ... have to be the change.

seven

KANYE

I remember exactly where I was when I heard that Kanye West had tweeted "I like the way Candace Owens thinks". It literally felt as though electricity was flowing through my entire being! You see, I saw that tweet as something I believed was going to have a massive impact on the Black community. Regardless of what you personally think about Kanye West or his music, he is an absolute hip hop icon, a legend, and thus a leader, for the Black community. I saw what I felt was a shockwave that had been emitted into the atmosphere, and that shockwave was going to have a ripple effect that would last for generations. Let me first say that I'm not a huge Kanye fan. His lyrics are drenched with vulgar and explicit themes and degrading talk about women, about drugs, and are filled with language of which I don't personally normally partake of myself. However, this is not about me. This current message that he had decided to champion was one that I could get behind. I've admired and appreciated his ability to rise above the tragedy that he went through, he almost died in a car accident. He came out after the accident and wrote a song about it. Initially, he had to record one of his first songs with his jaw wired shut.

73

I appreciated the fact that one of his first hits was a song called "Jesus Walks", and, believe it or not, I felt, and still feel, God speaking through Kanye in that song (yes, even though the song is laced with some foul language). I believe God can move through and speak through imperfect individuals, and even use them mightily for His ultimate purposes.

I've had the opportunity to watch Candace Owens rise to stardom, from becoming a Youtube personality to taking on a center-stage role in politics in the mainstream media. I was inspired by her thought-provoking videos that challenged the status quo about being Black and a Democrat. She has continually challenged what has been the norm amongst over 90 percent of the Black community for decades (the norm being that "all Blacks have to vote Democrat"). She's challenged this narrative over and over again from many different angles throughout her video series entitled *"Myth of the Coon"*. I saw her as a champion for the Black community, leading the charge for free thought, highlighting the value of thinking for oneself, regardless of skin color or what your parents have always told you.

I've seen her in debates where she tackled tough questions, and handled them with class and intelligence. So, understanding who I believed Candace Owens to be, and who I felt that she was to the Black community (literally the tip of the spear in the charge towards freeing Black America from the chains of bondage to a blind allegiance to any political party), when I heard that Kanye West had tweeted, "I like the way Candace Owens thinks", it sent shock waves through my body. I felt that what had transpired from that tweet was a catalyst for a new civil rights movement - a movement of Black people, for Black people - and I felt that this movement would garner the attention and support of Americans from all across the country.

Right after I heard about his tweet, I went to Kanye West radio on Spotify to see what came on. The very first song that played, out of the thousands of songs that Kanye West has recorded, was a song that starts out with the voice of a little 4-year-old girl praying. Her name is

Natalie, and this is what she says…

"Jesus! Praise the Lord! Hallelujah God! We don't want no devils in the house, God! We want the Lord!"

Are You Kidding Me!?!?! CHILLS!!! I felt shockwaves flooding through my body all over again… and they increased and continued as I listened to the entirety of that song!! To me, this was a sign that God was working in this entire Kanye West tweet. I listened to that song, bewildered that out of all the songs that could have come on, it was that one, "Ultralight Beam", and I felt God's presence so strongly that it was undeniable. Here's some of what Kanye says in that song…

"I'm tryna keep my faith
We on an ultralight beam
We on an ultralight beam
This is a God dream
This is a God dream
This is everything
This is everything
Deliver us serenity
Deliver us peace
Deliver us loving
We know we need it
You know we need it
You know we need it
That's why we need you now…"[69]

He was praying! To me, this is Kanye reaching out to God! One thing I do know about my Papa is that He loves to answer when we call out to Him. He may not answer when we want Him to, but He will *always* answer! That song was the one I was meant to hear in that moment. To me it was Papa - confirming what I had felt was transpiring - and I wept.

I then went to *Kanyewest.com* to see what was on his website, as I had never been there before. His website was very different than anything you think you'd see on a multi-platinum recording artist's website. It was very interesting looking. There was no normal banner or header, no pictures, nothing on the website whatsoever that said anything about Kanye or that even made it look like a normal website. There were two audio mp3's on an entirely blank white background. So, I clicked and played the first mp3. It was a song with Kanye West going back and forth with Rapper TI. In the song, TI (a black hip hop artist and actor) is basically telling Kanye that he's crazy for coming out in support of a man that's a racist, and Kanye is sharing why he believes enough in Donald Trump to come out in support of him. This was on the front of Kanye's website for the whole world to see!

This further cemented my belief that what I was feeling in my spirit, and what I was seeing unfold before my eyes, was indeed a movement that would become a great awakening in Black America.

I've heard that Kanye was told by several friends and mentors that if he came out in support of Donald Trump openly, it would end his career as a performer, as an entertainer, and as an artist. I also heard that when Kanye West made that tweet about Candace, it was the first tweet he had made in 18 months. He had remained completely silent on social media for that long. I wonder (and this is pure speculation on my part) if during those 18 months, I wonder if he was wrestling with those warnings from his friends telling him to not speak up, and if he was battling the fear of the consequences that might result from his sharing what he believed.

I wonder if part of the internal struggle that was trying to keep him pinned down was shame. You have to understand that over 90% of the black community has been spoon-fed since infancy the belief that Republicans hate black people. Then with the election, Trump was made out to look like the Grand Wizard of the KKK himself! So to come out openly supporting Donald Trump would feel like a slap in the face to most all of his friends and family.

Or, was it fear?

To openly come out in opposition to an ideology that the majority of Black Americans think could cost everything he'd spent a lifetime building. It had to be one of the hardest decisions he's ever had to make, knowing that he might be met with hatred and potentially, violence. I wonder if during that 18-month period of silence to all of his 28 million followers on Twitter, I wonder if God was speaking to Kanye... trying to encourage him, inspire him, or give him peace about sharing what was on his heart. Or, I wonder if what he saw taking place in front of him - the constant barrage of hate and animosity towards Donald Trump - was too much to handle, and that he ultimately decided that he, couldn't stay silent...

I absolutely believe that part of what I feel is the new civil rights movement was birthed during that 18-month period where Kanye West was silent on Twitter. It was birthed in how Candace Owens rose from being a Youtube sensation to an almost-daily Fox News contributor and analyst. I believe it was birthed in the heart of a young man named Charlie Kirk, the founder of an organization called Turning Point USA, who has made it his mission to educate the youth of America from high school to college and beyond on the facts of socialism and free market capitalism, and the strategies used to divide the races. I believe that it was birthed in the heart of Brandon Straka, founder of the #WalkAway Campaign that has opened the eyes of hundreds of thousands of people around the country, from all backgrounds, races, and creeds, to *Walk Away* from a political ideology that demands blind loyalty - the Democrat Party. I believe that the new civil rights movement has been birthed and cultivated in the hearts and minds of millions of Americans around the country right now - individuals like you, that are reading this book, and will take action by either passing it on to somebody else, or sharing a few copies with friends or individuals that may still be on that mental plantation, chained to emotions of hate and animosity instead of anchored to facts and rooted in love one for another.

eight

BLACK UNEMPLOYMENT

P resident Donald Trump's approval rating among Black voters has risen to heights rarely seen for a Republican President. It's nearly doubled in the span of a year's time.

Right now, Rasmussen's Daily Presidential Tracking Poll[70] shows Trump's approval rating with Black voters at 36 percent, compared to only 19 percent on the same day last year.

The spike in support didn't happen by Trump pandering to the Black community or by using racial platitudes. We simply like what his economic policies are doing for us. How can we not, with record low Black unemployment[71] and a booming economy which promises good economic times in the future?

That's something Democrats have always promised the Black community. They've done it ever since the days of FDR, and they never came through. In fact, FDR needed the racist wing of the Democratic Party in Congress to pass his New Deal legislation. They told FDR they wanted two things for their support. The first was that he was to block all anti-lynching legislation, to which he agreed. The next was that Blacks could not enjoy the benefits of his New Deal policies.

Guess what? The Democratic president again agreed! They told him that most Blacks back then worked in the residential services industry, so he excluded those jobs from Social Security. FDR[72] promised the Black community jobs in their cities for their support, and in the end, the jobs they got were temporary jobs building the highway bypass roads and ramps that allowed white people to drive through those neighborhoods to get to the real jobs found inside the cities.

Donald Trump didn't pull those kinds of racist stunts. He made a promise to the Black community, and if elected, he would do everything he could to help our communities. These polling numbers show that he is getting some recognition for coming through for us. Black Americans living in big cities still have many obstacles to overcome each and every day. The reason? Because Democrats still run everything at the local level.

Progressive Democrat policies make it difficult for people living in big cities to start a business, send their kids to a decent school, or afford to live in a nice neighborhood, even with the increase in salary from the Trump tax cuts. Progressives still control every aspect of life in major metropolitan areas. Who knows, maybe that too will start to change.

The approval numbers are even more extraordinary when you consider Trump's disheartening performance with Black voters during the 2016 election. There, he picked up only eight percent of Black men and four percent of Black women. These new numbers show that the Black community gave him a shot, and we have been paying attention ever since.

The same poll data shows Trump's overall approval rating at 49 percent of likely voters for his job performance, and 49 percent who will never approve of him, no matter how great America gets.

These figures also reveal that Trump is shrugging off accusations of racism from Democrats and the progressive left. Republicans are *always* going to be accused of racism from the Left. It's their playbook. How Republicans respond to those accusations makes all the difference. Normally, Republicans cower in the face of racism accusations, even when they know they've done nothing wrong. It's what I call Battered Republican Syndrome, where they panic at even false accusations, because Republicans not only have to deal with their own constituents and the opposing party, but a Democrat-supportive establishment news media that acts like the stenographers of the Democratic Party, along with left-leaning Hollywood and leftist academia.

Donald Trump *is* making America great again, and he includes all Americans in the effort.

As an American, and as a part of the Black community, I could not adequately express how excited this makes me! These numbers show not just that the mainstream media's lies are being exposed, and that the Black community is waking up, but it proves that when you fight for the truth, you will win!

I personally do not believe that Donald Trump's approval rating among the Black community would be as high as it is if it were not for real freedom fighters like Candace Owens. Her consistent exposure of the liberal hypocrisy, and Democrat lies that have maintained a hold on the Black community, have been showcased all over television, social media, and at events around the country. She is a leading and prominent voice for conservatives, and as a young Black woman, she gives an alternative perspective to young Black girls different from what they most likely have grown up hearing throughout their whole lives.

It's also because of strong Black women like Diamond and Silk that have held a steady course in the pursuit to wake Black America up. With truth and humor, they have reached beyond the scope of what most in journalism or in the news can do.

It's because of individuals like Brandon Tatum, a lifelong Democrat who decided to challenge the media narrative, and who actually attended a Trump rally. At that rally he encountered something that changed his life forever. He encountered caring and peaceful individuals. He encountered patriots that love their country and the freedoms that our country gives us. He saw firsthand how CNN later showed clips of attendees at the same rally that he attended, showing only white faces in the crowd behind Trump. Knowing that there were a lot of other races represented at that rally, he recognized the lies and the spin the mainstream media puts on their news to construct their biased narrative to fit what they want the people to believe. He woke up, he walked away, and he's shared video of his experiences, videos that have been viewed by over 70 million people, including President Trump! Donald Trump reached out to Brandon, and sent a bunch of MAGA gear to the police station where Brandon worked at the time.

Brandon was recently on Fox and Friends, and was asked to give his input on the NFL players kneeling, and about his support for Donald Trump. That clip was shared on Twitter by none other than Kanye West.

I believe it is because of Kanye West, a superstar, an icon, and a hip-hop legend, who was told to not come out about his positive feelings for Trump. He was told that it would ruin his career. He was told that he would be Blackballed and excommunicated from the hip-hop community. He was challenged, intimidated, and told to stay in his place. But he recognized that the place to which he was being restricted was actually a "plantation". He decided to go against all that advice, and after 18 months of silence on Twitter, came out in support of Donald J. Trump by showing his support for Candace Owens. The world responded! His latest album release became the #1 selling album in 81 countries! I don't think he truly understands how monumental that tweet was. I truly believe that that tweet gave Black America permission to think for themselves. It challenged the message that has been ingrained in many of us in the Black community from the time we were born.

I believe it's because of individuals like Brandon Straka, the founder of the #WalkAway Campaign, a lifelong liberal that cried when Donald Trump was elected president. He posted videos, ranting and sharing his inept disgust at how so many Americans could vote for such a man. Being a part of the gay community, he was surrounded by other liberals that believed Republicans are the enemy of freedom, peace, and love. Then one day a friend sent him a video that shattered the narrative that he held so dear. He shared his experience and the truth to which he had awakened to, and started a campaign that has changed hundreds of thousands of lives around the country. His story has given people permission to wake up and #WalkAway.

These are just a few of the real heroes that have laid their lives on the line to fight for freedom - and there are so many more. These approval numbers reflect the efforts of so many among the Latino community, the Asian community, and of Americans of all backgrounds that have joined forces to shine a spotlight on what I believe is one of the worst plagues to ever hit the soul of America. The Democrat party is being exposed. Their lies are being exposed. Truth is prevailing, and America will never be the same.

However, our fight is not over. It has just begun... As Harriet Tubman, who is famous for freeing thousands of slaves, said, "I freed a thousand slaves, and I could have freed a thousand more, if they only knew they were slaves.

nine

WHAT I BELIEVE

L et me be frank with you for a minute and just be myself. I understand that not all of you reading this book believe the way I do, but please allow me the latitude to share with you what I believe. I think that you'll find that no matter what your beliefs are about God, what we both think about life, hope, and love, are probably pretty similar. Maybe you'll read something that's new to you, and may even give you a different perspective on the matter.

I never knew that you had to identify as a conservative if you were also a Christian. I didn't realize there was any other kind. I grew up with Christian parents that brought me to church on Sundays and then sought to practice what they believed throughout the week. It was kindness to others. It was honesty, integrity, and truthfulness. It was loving people, and loving God, and seeking his will for your life.

It was believing that you were created for a purpose, and that there were specific tasks that you were placed on this earth to accomplish. While I believe that we can achieve some amazing things on our own, I believe that if we are not allowing input from Heaven into our lives, we miss out on what Papa dreamed about when He created us. For I believe that he saw questions that needed to be answered on Earth, and needs that needed to be met, and then he carefully handcrafted our innermost parts and wrapped our body around that dream. Or, let me put it like this… God had a dream, and then he wrapped your body around it…

While I believe that we all have talents and gifts, I also believe that when we ask God why he gave us those talents and gifts, we invite Heaven to participate in the journey of those talents as they unfold. When they do, we often see things happen by coincidence, at the right place, at the right time, and BOOM! Your talent just met face-to-face with an opportunity that not only aligned with your skills and passions, but aligned with Heaven's as well. I personally believe "coincidence" equals the language of the Spirit. I believe there is no "coincidence" with God. He is the master weaver and orchestrator who is able to bring things together that might otherwise seem impossible.

So I believe that when we invite Papa (God) into our lives, then when we work, are working hand-in-hand with the Creator of the universe.

I believe that Jesus, in Hebrew, Yeshua, is who He said He was. I believe that his story, the one told to us through that ancient text, is a story of love… He said some pretty outrageous things while he walked on this planet, and you don't have to have faith to believe that he actually existed. The man named Yeshua is in encyclopedias and in history books all around the world. The real question is, "is he who he said he was…"?

He said things like, "I am the way, the truth and the life, and no one can come to the Father but through me". So, Jesus was actually making the claim that he is the only way a person can get to The Father, who is in Heaven. That may sound outlandish, and even egotistical, unless you understand the true love story that is the Bible.

The Bible is comprised of 66 books, written by 40 different writers, all over a span of time of 1,500 years, and yet it is so harmoniously in sync with itself from beginning to end that is practically impossible to assume that all of these writers were able to create something aligning with one common theme. It's just humanly impossible, unless there was a supernatural force that filled them and gave them the inspiration to write the messages they wrote. Peter tried to explain this phenomenon in his second letter, the first chapter, 21st verse… "Holy men of God spoke as they were moved by God's Spirit". What he was literally suggesting is that God was the writer, and he used man as his writing instrument.

Therefore, God is the author of the book. That really is the only way to explain how from beginning to end, this book of letters could all share the same singular message. That message is not one that anybody, regardless of faith or belief, would really have to make any large leaps to believe. It's a message that says we live in a fallen world, a world that is filled with evil, a world that is filled with heartache and trauma from evil men trying to do evil things.

The message is that God is love.[73] God is perfect and pure. Think about that for a second. Pure love. Think about how hard we all try to love one another, and love ourselves, love our families, our spouses, and our children, yet we fall so short so often. But, we are still trying to love. To think about and try to comprehend what pure love must look like, how powerful and pure the makeup of love must be, is almost incomprehensible. Yet that's exactly what Jesus came to embody. Pure Love.

The truth is, love and hate do not mix, kind of like water and oil. If you love your family, if you love your friends, if you love your spouse, you wouldn't do anything intentionally to harm or hurt them. Love and hate cannot occupy the same space. They're not compatible.

So, let's look at love as pure light, if you will, and hate or evil, as darkness. There's absolutely no way that darkness can ever have a connection with pure light. So if we agree that there is no way that darkness can have connection with light, and we refer to the hate and evil in the world, and the wrongs that people do as darkness, then there is no way for that darkness to ever have a true connection with light.

The ultimate message of the letters that have been written that comprise that great ancient book we call the *Bible*, are letters that tell a story that God knew we would have no access to Him without some way to reconnect to Him. We live in a world where there are consequences for our actions. Break the law, and you have to pay a penalty. The universe is the same. Break the law of love, and a penalty must be paid. There must be some type of atonement made for our dark deeds; some type of sacrifice, paying atonement for the price for those wrongs, for that evil, for that sin. I believe that God devised a plan to redeem mankind from evil, and created a way for man to have an open and loving connection with Him, where the darkness that exists in our hearts doesn't keep us from having a connection with Him. That plan required a sacrifice, and God's Son willingly accepted the role of being that sacrifice.

THE VIRGIN BIRTH

The entire reason of the controversial and immaculate virgin birth makes sense if you understand the need for a perfect sacrifice. In order for Jesus to be that sacrifice, he had to be untainted from the very thing of which he was seeking to become the ransom for. I believe that sins are passed down to the next generation through the blood. That's why you can see in family trees, lines of abuse, alcoholism, or addictions, that go from one generation to the next to the next. This is the reason that Jesus had to be born of a virgin, to enable a human being to be born absolutely without sin. Here is an interesting fact about how the woman's body was created. Science has proven that a woman's body is able to grow and nurture a baby inside the womb without ever having the mother's blood intermingle with the baby's blood. Dr. Gerard M. Dileo explains it like this

"The placenta is part of the communication between the fetus and the expectant mother. Most people tend to think of this communication as the route of exchange where the mother's blood and the fetus's blood mix and exchange, but this is a myth. The fetal blood and maternal blood do not mix. In fact, if this were to be the case, there would be such immunological protest from the mother that she would soon deliver enough antibodies into the baby's blood to destroy the pregnancy."[74]

So the reason for the virgin birth would have to be by very intelligent design. Mary, "the virgin" literally became pregnant because God's presence rested on her, and his seed was placed inside her. It's important to note that Mary was a willing participant. An angel showed up and announced it to her. He gave her the option to refuse, but she was more than willing! Who wouldn't be! To be impregnated by the Creator of the Universe? Are You Kidding Me!?!?! What an honor! She said yes, God's seed was planted, and a human with Gods DNA was created. Because of the miraculous nature of the way in which his blood was not mixed with his mother's, he was born without sin. He was born pure, like the original Adam God created.

I believe the book comprised of the letters that were written, by all those different authors, all share a message of how God created the universe. In that universe, he created earth, and on that planet, he created beings that would have the opportunity to have friendship with Him. I believe God wanted a friend. I believe God wanted to pour his love into another being so much so that he created mankind and said, "The world is yours". I also believe that the ultimate gift he gave mankind was the gift of free will. We are not robots. We are not all programmed to all do the same thing, or love and honor Him out of demand. We all have thousands of choices to make every single day that make up who we are… and we are the ones that get to choose how we interact with others, how we love others, and hopefully, our ultimate goal is to love others well.

I believe God wanted to love us, and He wanted to be able to be loved by us. But I also believe that He's omniscient. Even before he gave those first humans free will, he foresaw that free will would open the door to evil. He saw that if He created mankind with the ability to choose, it would open the door to a problem; sin. And sin breeds evil. Evil by definition means: profoundly immoral and malevolent; harmful or tending to cause harm; extremely unpleasant. Sin is the word used to describe the evil that lurks in our blood.

Since Adam and Eve were had crafted by God, and His breath is what gave them life, they were perfect. They were pure. For God to give them free will, would mean He would have to give them access to something outside of His perfection, outside of Love, of which they could choose. So he put a tree called The Knowledge of Good and Evil in their garden and instructed them not to eat its fruit. The fruit, if consumed, would open their hearts and minds to the knowledge of, thoughts of, evil. And of that evil, we have seen the extents of its desires displayed throughout the centuries. While telling a lie may seem innocent, it's the same pathway that liars will use to cheat, steal, and even kill. It comes from the same vein. Have you ever had a crazy thought about someone else or yourself? Something that you wouldn't act on, but still the thought popped in your head anyways?

"What if I drove my car off that cliff?"

Someone cuts you off while driving, "man I'd like to ram their car"

Or thoughts of causing real physical damage, pain or even death to someone or ourselves? I know I have in my lifetime... Even though we may never act on those thoughts, the fact that they are there, is evidence that evil lurks in our blood. For some people do act on those thoughts. And nefarious things occur. I believe evil entered into our blood when Adam and Eve consumed that fruit. The Knowledge of Evil... The "thoughts" of evil... And that evil, would have to be conquered if we were to be able to have true fellowship with God. With Love.

Adam ate the fruit and sin arrived on the scene. Choosing to do things our own way and not trust our Creator, would open the door those actions growing more and more evil and dark. This sin, would get passed down through the blood infecting every human that would ever be born.

Sin also stole our identity. It's interesting that as soon as Adam and Eve did what God told them not to do, they immediately became self-conscience. Understand they were created naked, walked around naked, and never once had an awareness of it. As soon as they ate the fruit that God had instructed them not to eat, they immediately became self-conscience of the fact that they were naked. I believe that sin steals our identity. We were created to live, walk, and be perfect. An absolute reflection of the One that created us. When sin entered in, we lost the ability to reflect that perfection on our own. And that problem would require what only a perfect sacrifice would be able to solve.

Therefore, I believe the love story of the Bible is that God's Son accepted the responsibility to come down to Earth, to be born of a virgin, of the seed of his Father. His mission was to live a perfectly pure life, and to live listening to, and leaning into, his Father. It is recorded that Jesus said, "I only say what I hear my Father saying, and do what I see my Father doing". He was modeling what having a relationship with the Father could look like. I don't care what you believe, find me one thing that Jesus did that was recorded in the scriptures that wasn't either full of compassion or miraculous! Jesus also understood that at the end of His life, He would have to be that sacrifice.

It has been written that when Jesus was praying the night before his crucifixion, he prayed for hours. He prayed so hard that drops of blood were literally coming out of the pores of his head. He understood the absolute torture that he was about to endure, and he asked, he *begged*, "Father, if you are willing, please take this cup of suffering away from me. Yet I want your will to be done, not mine." Ultimately, he knew there was only one way to redeem mankind.

You see, no matter how many people are in this world, if you believe those ancient texts as I do, this world was populated by one man,
Adam, and his bride Eve. Therefore, it was the actions of one man that
opened the door to the darkness that plagues humanity, and therefore
it only took the actions of one perfect and pure man to pay the price for
that darkness and redeem humanity.

THE PRICE HE PAID

The accounts that were recorded about how Jesus looked after he was
beaten and whipped the day of his crucifixion are astonishingly horrific. Isaiah wrote in one of his letters that he had seen a vision of the re-
deemer. He saw what Jesus looked like after he had endured the torture
and whippings before he went to the cross. He said that his image was
so marred and disfigured that he did not look like a man, and his form
did not resemble a human being. (CSB Isaiah 52:14)

You see, the Romans had perfected the art of whipping a prisoner.
David McClister gives us a good look into what Jesus went through
leading up to his crucifixion.

> *"The Crucifixion was an agonizing, torturous death, but
> Jesus endured a torture that was nearly as, or perhaps equally,
> excruciating before he ever got to the cross. This was the pain he
> suffered when he was scourged.*
>
> *Scourging, called verberatio by the Romans, was possibly
> the worst kind of flogging administered by ancient courts. While
> the Jews administered whippings in the synagogues for certain
> offenses, these were mild in comparison to scourging. Scourging
> was not normally a form of execution, but it certainly was bru-
> tal enough to be fatal in many cases. A person certainly could
> be beaten to death by the scourge if that was desired. Its purpose
> was not only to cause great pain, but to humiliate as well. To
> scourge a man was to beat him worse than one would beat a*

stupid animal. It was belittling, debasing, and demeaning. It was considered such a degrading form of punishment that, according to the Porcian (248 B.C.) and Sempronian (123 B.C.) laws, Roman citizens were exempt from it. It was, therefore, the punishment appropriate only for slaves and non-Romans, those who were viewed as the lesser elements in Roman society. To make it as humiliating as possible, scourging was carried out in public.

The instrument used to deliver this form of punishment was called in Latin a flagellum or a flagrum. This was much different from the bull whip that is more common in our culture. It was instead more like the old British cat o' nine tails, except that the flagellum was not designed merely to bruise or leave welts on the victim. The flagellum was a whip with several (at least three) thongs or strands, each perhaps as much as three feet long, and the strands were weighted with lead balls or pieces of bone. This instrument was designed to lacerate. The weighed thongs struck the skin so violently that it broke open. The church historian Eusebius of Caesarea recounts with vivid, horrible detail a scene of scourging. He says, "For they say that the bystanders were struck with amazement when they saw them lacerated with scourges even to the innermost veins and arteries, so that the hidden inward parts of the body, both their bowels and their members, were exposed to view" (Ecclesiastical History, Book 4, chap. 15).

The victim of a scourging was bound to a post or frame, stripped of his clothing, and beaten with the flagellum from the shoulders to the loins. The beating left the victim bloody and weak, in unimaginable pain, and near the point of death. It is no doubt that weakness from his scourging was largely the reason Jesus was unable to carry his cross all the way to Golgotha[75] (Matt. 27:32 and parallels)."

After weaving branches containing long thorns into a circle, they shoved it down on top of Jesus head, causing the skin and the flesh to tear open and bleed. And, after all this, they placed a robe on his blood-drenched body, allowing the blood to absorb into the robe, knowing that as it dried, when they would eventually have to rip the robe off, when it would then tear any dried blood off and tear the skin off with it.

They made him carry his own cross, a tree on which he was to be hung, throughout the city to be ridiculed, mocked and spit on. Somewhere along his journey to his ultimate place of death, his legs buckled from the weight of the tree, and he could not keep moving. That's where a guard ordered a man named Simon to carry his cross. It's interesting to me that Simon[76] was from Cyrene. Cyrene was a city located in Africa. That seems to indicate quite clearly that Simon was a man from Africa, a Black man, that helped to carry the cross of Christ.

After he had been nailed through both wrists and both feet to the tree, they stood the tree up and let it fall down into the hole. I'm sure the pressure of his body weight caused a severe, jarring jolt when the tree hit the bottom of that hole. There he hung… a man that had spoken love and performed miracles, and had continually spoken about the love of his Father for all mankind. There he was, hanging nailed to a tree…

To think about the fact, that he was hanging on a tree, on something that he had created for the beauty and the enjoyment of his creation, is just beyond imagination… and he was nailed to that tree by the very creation he made for Him to love! What ultimate betrayal he must have felt. What ultimate dismay he must have endured on top of the physical torture. On top of the emotional torture, he had to endure the humiliation and betrayal at the hands of the very beings that he had created to love… and yet he willingly did all this, for you, and for me.

There were billions of angels focused on nothing else that day. I bet they were watching, eagerly anticipating, waiting for their Creator to give them the okay to free him from that tree, and to kill every single person that had put him there. I bet they waited intently, perhaps actually hoping that he would give the word so that they would not have to witness their beloved Creator being tortured.

Jesus did open his mouth… and said, "Father, forgive them, for they don't know what they are doing". Even feeling the weight of betrayal, torture and humiliation, Pure Love still said, "Forgive them". That is pure love. That is love.

I believe no human has ever been born, not before him, and not since, that is capable of enduring what he endured and still have what it took to still be speak and act with love. What we see here *is* the embodiment of love.

The accounts written of the moments right after he took his final breath say that there was lightning in the sky, and a rumbling of the earth as if the world was ending. It's even written that some of the soldiers who mocked him as being the Son of God, after witnessing what took place in the sky, changed their tune and said, "This man truly was the Son of God!" Matt 27:54

You see, the message of the Bible is a love story, a story that explains why he willing went through it all. It says "for the joy that was laid before him, he endured the cross, despising the shame…" Heb 12:2 I believe the joy that he saw just beyond the torture, the joy he saw beyond the humiliation, the joy that he saw passed all of the pain… was *you*. It was *me*.

He saw his original intended purpose of loving us, and us loving him, being restored. He saw the ability to have a truly intimate connection with the very creation he designed. I believe that it was because he saw us that made it possible for him to endure the cross. It is a love story. Jesus's life is a love story to mankind. Even in his death, it speaks and shouts "I LOVE YOU!!!"

The story of his resurrection is a story of him defeating everything that could ever come against us in our life, even the event that so many of us dread, death. He defeated it. I believe him rising from the grave again says "Not even death will have a hold on those that I love and that believe in me". That is what I believe. That is why I am a believer.

A CONSERVATIVE CHRISTIAN

I think that while there can be several issues on which Christians can hold a difference of opinion regarding party lines, the one major issue that separates conservatives from liberals is their value for an unborn human life. A person has to choose to not see a growing baby inside the womb of a mother as a life in order to justify ending that life. Here are a couple verses that you would have to tear out of the Bible if, as a Christian, you were going to feel comfortable with killing an unborn baby.

Jeremiah wrote in the first chapter of his book, the fifth verse, inspired by what he felt God had shown him: "Before I formed you in the womb I knew you ... and I appointed you a prophet to the nations." To me this says that the man that walked and lived on the earth named Jeremiah had an identity that was recognized while he was still in his mother's womb. By declaring that he was "appointed" as a prophet tells me that God had plans for his existence on earth. All of this points to life - To existence - To belonging.

More verses that speak to existing with purpose while still inside the womb are in the book of Psalms, chapter 139, verses 13-16, where it says...

"For you created my inmost being; you knit me together in my mother's womb. I praise you because I am fearfully and wonderfully made; your works are wonderful, I know that full well. My frame was not hidden from you when I was made in the secret place, when I was woven together in the depths of the earth. Your eyes saw my unformed body; all the days ordained for me were written in your book before one of them came to be."

As a Christian, if I believe this verse in the Bible which says that "I" was "knit together" in my mother's womb, then how could I *dare* justify ending the life of a baby that's inside the womb? That verse ends with "all the days ordained for me were written in your book, before even one of them came to be"! Are you kidding me!? This speaks to existence - existing while still in the womb! I don't know about you, but that gets me excited about life!

So if the main argument for abortion is that it's only tissue inside a woman's body, and it's not a life yet, how could a Christian that loves God and his book of promises justify ending the life of an unborn child? That totally baffles me. The Democrat party pushes for abortion. They are okay with partial-birth abortion, which is where the doctor literally has to use metal forceps to reach inside the womb and break the bones of the baby in order to tear pieces of the baby out one by one... a grotesque and inhumane way to die! Putting a person to death by tearing them limb from limb would *never* be considered outside of the womb.

The fact that there are so many Christians that support the Democrat party's platform is unbelievable to me... and yet, it's the truth. If there were one reason, and one reason alone, for believers to support conservative candidates, it would be his or her stance on abortion. I believe that no other issue is more paramount to the health of the soul of a country, or of an individual, than the willingness to choose life, and not support the death of our most precious gifts from Heaven...

The discussion of abortion also hits very close to home for me, for I would not be the man I am today had abortion had its way. Soon after that third Presidential debate between Trump and Hillary in 2016, my bride felt compelled to open up and publicly share something that was very personal to her and very few people knew...

ten

WHY JENNIFER COULDN'T STAY SILENT

"Hello. Would you allow me a few minutes of your time, enough time to share something pressing with you....?

My name is Jennifer. In 1977 my mother scheduled an appointment to terminate me. Some would merely sluff this off as her right to abort an unborn baby, but actually, it was my LIFE. Did you hear me? There was an appointment to have me killed.

Let that sink in...

Praise God, my mom changed her mind at the last minute. She walked out of that clinic as a mother with newfound love for the child growing inside her. She was a single, beautiful, hurting, lost, pregnant woman. My Certificate of Birth has a checkmark next to "Father Withheld." (I finally met my dad for the first time when I was 10 years old, and established a relationship with him as an adult.) My mom's circumstances were not ideal by any means, but she still chose LIFE.

While I was still at elementary school age, I can remember my mom sharing with me that she had had an abortion before I was born.

She carried this sort of ...internalized... guilt. I can remember the way it looked on her face... Abortion can take its toll. My mom received Christ as her Savior, and soon turned that guilt into a strong stand for life. I can remember picketing with my mom in front of abortion clinics. She actually got arrested for hopping the fence of a local clinic. She wanted to have words with the ladies. She wanted to save lives.

Let me stop here and say this: His grace covers ALL the things. If you're reading this and you've had an abortion, there is no judgment here. Go to God if you haven't already - He's waiting for you. He is full of forgiveness and new beginnings! If you are with child and considering aborting your baby; the beautiful, tiny human growing rapidly inside of your womb, please reconsider. PLEASE! That baby in your womb deserves LIFE. That precious little baby has already been named by our Creator. There are so many options to help women who want to keep their babies but feel they need assistance, as well as options for mothers deciding adoption is the best fit for them. Regardless of how helpless your situation may seem, there is help out there. It wasn't until my mom was very sick that I learned I was supposed to be aborted. You can probably imagine the shock I felt. After the words sunk in for a brief minute, all I could say was, "Thank you for keeping me, mom." There was an awkward kind of silence in the room...

By this time, I had been married for five years and I was already a mama to two amazing little girls. Life was full. My mom was losing her battle to cancer, and there just wasn't time to really process what could have never been.

Fast forward 15 years. This election really has me thinking about the gift of life. I have been processing what could have never been.

My daughters are adults now. They're loving, wise, smart, beautiful, and witty ladies. What about them?! Where would they be without me? This life, MY life, has produced two World Changers. They are my flesh and blood. What about them?! They didn't even stand a chance without me. They matter too.

My daughters have been hand-picked for the Grand Master Plan. If I had been aborted, their destiny would've been sacrificed. Every. Single. Baby. From the minute of conception, every single one has a destiny. Please, fight for the sanctity of life!

It says in Psalm 139:15-16, "My frame was not hidden from you when I was made in the secret place, when I was woven together in the depths of the earth. Your eyes saw my unformed body; all the days ordained for me were written in your book before one of them came to be.

Political side note: This has not been an easy election for me. Heck, I doubt it's been easy for anyone. I have refrained from 99 percent of political conversation because I just wasn't happy with either choice. Once our nation was at a clear Trump-or-Hillary standstill, I wasn't wavering about who I was voting for, but I certainly wasn't laying out my choice publicly.

Until now.

Here's the deal: Donald Trump wants to save babies. He wants to fix our healthcare system. He wants to secure our borders and bring jobs back to America. He believes in pledging allegiance to the flag

We have two choices, people: Trump or Hillary. Please do your homework. I get it... Trump may not look like the president you imagined would take office to heal our country. Guess what? He loves America. He stands for the principles our nation was founded on.

I urge you to take the time to read, pray, and do your due diligence as an American voter. We have 7 days until we head to our designated polling place. America is crying out for help. We have help knocking at the presidential door; it's Trump.

In closing, I will say this: Words cannot express the happiness I feel that my mom decided to carry me and birth the LIFE that started in her womb! The life she offered me was far from perfect, but I wouldn't change it for anything.

For any woman who is undecided or considering abortion: *Do not* listen to the lie that you are not good enough, smart enough, well off enough, educated enough, loved enough, or in the right situation to be a mother. You have the CHOICE to make the best decision for your baby: keep your daughter or son, and give them the best life you can, or give them up, as a gift, to another family that is ready to take on parenting. With either of those decisions, you win, and, so does the baby! With abortion, there can only be hurt and loss.

Thank you for sharing time with me.

See you at the voting polls."

Her post was shared thousands of times. Messages began flooding in from women that had had an abortion, thanking her for not adding any shame or guilt. Messages came in from women that were contemplating an abortion that then decided not to have one. And then a year later, this message came in ...

"Hey David, I wanted to share something with you and Jennifer. Last year a dear friend of mine found herself in a very difficult situation and was seriously considering getting an abortion. She came to me because she knew I would talk her through it without judgment and would help her find the answer that was right for her. I knew without a doubt what the right thing to do was, but finding the words to bring her to see that as well was a greater challenge. I prayed for her and I prayed for God's guidance, and He came through in a big way, through you and Jennifer. That night I got on Facebook and in my feed came you sharing Jennifer's story about her mom having considered abortion and the impact of having walked out that day and the beautiful lives that exist today because of that. I shared that story with my friend and it solidified her decision to keep her baby. Sweet little Ian is full of smiles and joy thanks to you and Jennifer sharing her story. If you weren't sure that your presence online was making a difference, know that it very much is! Meet Ian!"

Wow! We read this, and sobbed... In deciding to not stay silent, and using our voices on the issue, to have aided in saving this one life... It was a miracle! God is So Good!!!

eleven

THE NEW KKK

I think it's important that we remember the agenda behind the Klu Klux Klan. The KKK was without a doubt, a private military militia-style arm of the Democrat Party, that sought to keep Black Americans from gaining any type of independence apart from them. The KKK was founded by Nathan Bedford Forrest, a Democrat, and was comprised of all Democrats. The KKK did absolutely inhumane and despicably evil things to Black individuals that sought their own freedom. It's crazy to me that so many Black Americans of today are unaware of these facts. The notion that somehow in the 1960's, all Democrats suddenly became the party fighting for the civil rights for Blacks is not only laughable, but unconscionable. For when there is that much hate inside of a person's heart (and we are literally talking about thousands, probably tens of thousands of individuals' hearts), a hate that was so abhorrent towards people of color, there's no way that all of those individuals suddenly had a change of heart and decided to start fighting for Black Americans. The KKK's role was to do *outside* of the law what couldn't be done *inside* the law. The KKK pushed to enforce Jim Crow laws, segregation laws, and laws that kept Blacks from mingling with whites in any type of loving capacity. They sought to control, manipulate, and dominate Black Americans.

In today's day and age, I'm sure there are still those with that level of hatred in their heart towards Black Americans, but there's no way they could pull off the type of violence that the KKK used to be able to get away with. I believe that there's a new KKK at work in our country that seeks to control, manipulate, and dominate not only the Black community, but anyone willing to obstruct their agenda. I believe it is spread across a variety of platforms and sectors. The continual push towards inflaming, or even creating, racial tensions has been exposed by how mainstream media outlets will push one narrative over another. Our mainstream media sources used to have a neutral journalistic approach to reporting the news. Now, I believe many of them have changed their narrative and direction of reporting to capitalize on or inflame issues of violence that they feel will stir up strife between the Black and White community.

Instances of this have been proven against a network that came in third in primetime viewership in January of 2018. CNN, whose tagline is "America's Most Trusted News Network", has been at the forefront of Donald Trump's accusations of being "fake news". While some pawn that off to "Well, that's because they're reporting *dirt* on him", I think it's important to evaluate the facts. Think about it for a second. What kind of power does our Most Trusted News Network hold over us if we believe them and never research what's proposed for ourselves?

Here's 18 times that mainstream media outlets were caught sharing fake news.

1. SCARAMUCCI SLIP

CNN retracted a story in June of 2016 claiming that former Trump adviser Anthony Scaramucci was under investigation by Congress for his alleged ties to Russia. The story relied on one anonymous congressional source and CNN apologized to Scaramucci for the error. Three CNN reporters ended up resigning from the company[77] over the botched report.

2. TRUMP JR. COLLUSION

CNN reported in December of 2017 that Donald Trump Jr. received special access to documents stolen by WikiLeaks on Sept. 4, 2016. However, Donald Trump Jr. actually was emailed about the documents on Sept. 14, 2016 — a day after they were already available to the general public. CNN updated the report but still has not explained how two sources managed to give them the wrong date on the email.

3. 17 INTEL AGENCIES LIE

Former Director of National Intelligence James Clapper said during a congressional hearing in May that three intelligence agencies — the CIA, NSA and the FBI — concluded that Russia interfered with the 2016 election.

Nonetheless, CNN has repeatedly claimed[78] that all 17 intelligence agencies[79] came to the same conclusion about Russian meddling. CNN's claim is pure nonsense, as the Department of Energy, Department of the Treasury, and Drug Enforcement Agency, among others, would have no authority to make any assertions about Russian meddling in elections.

4. COMEY TESTIMONY CRUMBLES

On June 6, 2017, CNN reported that former FBI director James Comey would contradict President Donald Trump's claim that he was not under investigation.

When the time came for Comey to release his opening statement for his congressional testimony, he actually ended up confirming Trump's account.

CNN corrected by saying this: "This article was published before Comey released his prepared opening statement. The article and headline have been corrected to reflect that Comey does not directly dispute that Trump was told multiple times he was not under investigation in his prepared testimony released after this story was published,"

5. TRUMP'S FISH FOOD

When President Trump met with Japanese Prime Minister Shinzo Abe last November, the pair took part in a koi fish feeding ceremony. A video posted by CNN appeared to show Trump dumping his entire box of food into the koi pond unprompted.

An unedited video revealed that Trump was simply following the lead of Abe, who emptied his box of food first.

6. A CLEAN BILL OF HEALTH

In May of 2017 when Republicans were authoring a new health care bill, CNN claimed[80] that GOP changes to Obamacare could make rape and sexual assault pre-existing conditions.

PolitiFact[81] rated that claim "mostly false," explaining that "the bill does not change what is or is not a pre-existing condition; the health insurance companies write those definitions for themselves."

7. OFFICER CUOMO

CNN anchor Chris Cuomo inexplicably said in October of 2016 that possessing WikiLeaks stolen documents is "illegal," but insisted it's "different for the media."

"Also interesting is, remember, it's illegal to possess these stolen documents. It's different for the media. So everything you learn about this, you're learning from us," Cuomo said

According to The Washington Post[82], it is not illegal to possess or distribute illegally obtained material so long as you were not involved in the original hack.

8. JUST TAP IT IN

CNN originally denounced Trump's claim in March of 2017 that former President Barack Obama was wiretapping phones in Trump Tower as a "flat-out lie."[83]

Then, in September of 2017, CNN reported that the FBI had a wiretap on former campaign chairman Paul Manafort — who has a residence in Trump Tower.

While it is unclear if the FBI tapped Manafort's phones in Trump Tower or picked up his conversations with the president, it's plausible enough that CNN should not be dismissing Trump's claims out of hand

9. ZELENY'S FOLLY

CNN reporter Jeff Zeleny tweeted on July 31, 2018, that President Trump had not taken questions from reporters in at least a week.

President Trump waves but declines to answer questions on south lawn of White House today as he heads to Florida for a campaign rally tonight. It marks at least a week that he's gone without answering questions about his Tweets or anything else in the news.

Just one day prior to Zeleny's tweet, Trump answered questions during a joint news conference[84] with the Italian Prime Minister Giuseppe Conte.

10. REPUBLICANS DID (NOT) FUND THE DOSSIER

The salacious and unverified Steele dossier was paid for by the Democratic National Committee and the Clinton campaign, but that hasn't stopped CNN from pinning the document on the GOP

Former Obama official and current CNN reporter Jim Sciutto was just one network talking-head who claimed the dossier was "initially paid for by Republicans."

While Republicans bought standard opposition research from Fusion GPS, they stopped paying the firm well before it ever contracted with Christopher Steele to compile the anti-Trump dossier.

11. IF YOU BUILD IT, THEY WILL LIE

CNN claimed that only Democratic members of Congress gathered to pray before the 2017 Congressional Baseball Game — the first game after House Majority Whip Steve Scalise was shot and nearly killed.

Pictures of the prayer circle clearly show both Democrats and Republicans praying together, and CNN eventually deleted their tweet claiming otherwise.

12. CNN GETS HIT WITH A CRUZ MISSILE

After the school shooting in Parkland, Florida, CNN media reporter Brian Stelter accused Republican congressmen of being "scared" to come on the network to debate gun control. Anchor Chris Cuomo specifically called out Texas Senator Ted Cruz for not rising to the challenge.

As it turns out, Sen. Cruz had done a 15 minute interview with CNN earlier that day. He blasted the network for airing "NONE" of his interview and noted that he had previously done three town hall debates on CNN with Senator Bernie Sanders.

13. SILLY STELTER!

CNN media reporter Brian Stelter accused the[85] Republican National Committee of "misquoting" him in an ad attacking the credibility of Michael Wolff's book "Fire and Fury."

"Real factual errors ... makes you wonder about the overall content," Stelter was quoted as saying.

Stelter did utter those words during a CNN International television hit and quickly deleted his accusatory tweet.

"I stand corrected: I thought this RNC ad misquoted me, but the quote came from a @CNNI TV hit. So I've deleted my previous tweet about this." Stelter admitted.

14. THESE BOOTS WERE MADE FOR CORRECTIN'

Nancy Sinatra made a quick joke about her late father's song, "My Way," being used at Trump's Inauguration in January 2017. She tweeted in response to the news to "just remember the first line of the song" — which is, "And now, the end is near."

CNN spun Sinatra's tweet[86] into an article claiming she was "not happy" about Trump using her father's song at the Inauguration.

"That's not true. I never said that. Why do you lie, CNN?" Sinatra asserted. "What a rotten spin to put on a harmless joke."

15. SCHOOL SHOOTING SLIP-UP

After a May shooting at Santa Fe High School in Texas, CNN reporters immediately began claiming that there were 22 school shootings on the year.

However, CNN wildly exaggerates the number of school shootings by using methodology that includes accidental firearm discharges on school property, domestic disputes, and other non-active shooter events.

For example, one listed shooting[87] at Savannah State University in Georgia involved just two people, neither of whom were students.

16. FAKE NEWS ABOUT FAKE NEWS

CNN cited a study from the Oxford Internet Institute to claim that fake news targeted swing states during the 2016 presidential election.

However, as The Daily Caller first reported, the study says nothing of the sort.

The researchers in the study were talking about "junk news," not "fake news" — and their definition of junk news includes mainstream conservative sites like The Washington Examiner and Breitbart News. A deep dive into the study thus reveals that Twitter users didn't receive nearly as much "fake news" as CNN initially claimed to readers.

17. HANDS UP, FAKE NEWS

A CNN panel consisting of Margaret Hoover, Sally Kohn, Sunny Hostin and Mel Robbins displayed the "hands up, don't shoot"[88] gesture in 2014 while talking about marches against police violence.

The gesture seemed to be a reference to the fatal police shooting of Michael Brown in Ferguson, Missouri.

While initial reports speculated that Brown had his hands up when he was shot by Darren Wilson, the DOJ concluded in a report[89] in 2015 that physical and forensic evidence showed Brown's hands could not have been above his waist.

18. PEACE BE WITH YOU

CNN deceptively edited a video of Sherelle Smith and Kimberly Neal, the sisters of an unarmed Black man who was shot by police. The network claimed the two sisters were "calling for peace" amidst riots in their neighborhood.

"Don't bring that violence here,' [Kimberly] Neal, his other sister, said while sobbing," CNN's report said.

However, in a longer video, Sherelle says, "Y'all burning down s—t we need in our community. Take that s—t to the suburbs. Burn that s—t down. We need our s—t. We need our weaves. I don't wear it. But we need it."

CNN removed the portion of their report about Sherelle and owned up to their error.

"An earlier version of this story mischaracterized what the victim's sister was trying to convey. She was calling for peace in her community, urging the protesters to go elsewhere," CNN told The Washington Examiner.[90]

A big thanks to Amber Athey and The Daily Caller for helping to put this fantastic list together.

While the majority of the above Fake News stories are comprised from CNN, NBC News has been busted for spreading a fake news as well. They published a conspiracy theory claiming that President Donald Trump and Justice Anthony Kennedy secretly worked together for months to find his replacement on the Supreme Court.

That is arguably the most fake of the fake news. The reporters "source" proves this was nothing more than an attempted smear job on the president.

In a now-deleted tweet, NBC's Leigh Ann Caldwell said on Tuesday morning that her "sources" said there was a secret Trump-Kennedy pact to help find his replacement on the High Court. Here's her first tweet:

On Kavanaugh pick Kennedy and Trump/WH had been in negotiations for months over Kennedy's replacement. Once Kennedy received assurances that it would be Kavanaugh, his former law clerk, Kennedy felt comfortable retiring, according to a source who was told of the discussions.

Then, she tweeted this:

Furthermore, the five names Trump added to his list of Federalist Approved judges last November was to get Kavanaugh on that list. The other four names were considered cover, per source. In other words: the decision has been baked for a while[.]

After getting put through the wringer on the claim, Caldwell admitted that her "scoop" was nothing more than a fake news conspiracy that she heard third-hand from another person.

She clarified in a follow-up post and deleted her original tweet:

I've deleted this tweet because it incorrectly implies a transactional nature in Kennedy's replacement. I am told by a source who was not directly part of the talks that Kennedy provided Pres. Trump/ WH a list of acceptable replacements. (1/2) pic.twitter.com/ptxJmrbH9S[91]

— Leigh Ann Caldwell (@LACaldwellDC)
July 10, 2018

To be clear: This is from one source and don't have any info on whether potus talked to kennedy about a possible replacement.

— Leigh Ann Caldwell (@LACaldwellDC)
July 10, 2018

At one point, these stations may have been trusted news networks, but after viewing this list, you'd have to ask yourself... are they actually intentionally trying to persuade their viewers to believe their narrative, regardless of the facts? Think about the power of persuasion that you would have over a large section of the country if you promoted yourself to be a trusted news network, yet your goal was to actually control, manipulate, and dominate the audience that you had. People used to read the paper as trusted news. They read the paper as information that just gave the facts, but somewhere along the line the powers that would like to divide our country and send our country into a totalitarian regime run by the ultra-elite, took over. Ninety percent of the news stations in the country are owned by just six corporations. In 1950, there were over 50 different companies that comprised the news and information we get.

The six corporations that collectively control U.S. media today are Time Warner, Walt Disney, Viacom, Rupert Murdoch's News Corp., CBS Corporation, and NBC Universal. Together, the "big six" absolutely dominate news and entertainment in the United States. But even those areas of the media that the "big six" do not completely control are becoming increasingly concentrated. For example, Clear Channel now owns over 1,000 radio stations across the United States. Companies like Google, Yahoo and Microsoft are increasingly dominating the Internet.

When you control what Americans watch, hear, and read you gain a great deal of control over what they think. They don't call it "programming" for nothing!

Back in 1983 it was bad enough that about 50 corporations dominated the U.S. media. But since that time, power over the media has rapidly become concentrated in the hands of fewer and fewer people....

In 1983, fifty corporations dominated most of every mass medium and the biggest media merger in history was a $340

million deal. ... [I]n 1987, the fifty companies had shrunk
to twenty-nine. ... [I]n 1990, the twenty-nine had shrunk to
twenty-three. ... [I]n 1997, the biggest firms numbered ten
and involved the $19 billion Disney-ABC deal, at the time the
biggest media merger ever. ... [In 2000] AOL Time Warner's
$350 billion merged corporation [was] more than 1,000 times
larger [than the biggest deal of 1983].

–Ben H. Bagdikian, The Media Monopoly[92], Sixth Edi-
tion, (Beacon Press, 2000), pp. xx—xxi

This should tell you something. What are these group's intentions? What are their philosophies? What do they hope to achieve by what they are reporting? I believe it is important in this day and age in which we live, where news is readily available to us from thousands of different sources every day, that we understand where those sources come from, and what agenda they may have in their reporting. I believe that the new KKK seeks to control, manipulate, and dominate in ways that are just as divisive. They may not be as physically harmful, but they are still seeking to control the masses that they seek to dominate with their power.

In the world of social media, over which I've been building my brand over the last year and a half, I have been a victim of such divisiveness and control. I'm very obviously an outspoken individual when it comes to current affairs, politics, and my beliefs about what is taking place in our country. I do not fit the narrative that is continually being pushed on the masses, the one that says that the Democrat Party is the party for Black Americans. I don't buy into the narrative that has been painted about Donald Trump being a sexist, misogynist, and a bigot, and that's why Blacks need to hate him. Since I don't fit that narrative, that's why I believe I have felt the weight of the new KKK around my neck trying to silence me, trying to limit my ability to reach others with what I believe is the truth, ultimately trying to take away my First Amendment right in sharing the truths and exposing the lies I have uncovered.

I believe the heart and spirit behind the hate, control and divisiveness of the original KKK is still at work in America today through media, social media companies, and journalists that seek to align with that totalitarian agenda.

In January of 2018, I had a little over 200,000 followers on Facebook. I had just started my website, DavidHarrisJr.com, and had contracted writers that would research topics and deliver the information that I believe was unbiased, and would try to expose the lies and share the truth. My website was getting over 500,000 visitors within its first couple of months, and I wanted to take my platform to a new level on Facebook.

Facebook has a monetization feature for individuals or pages on their platform that enables them to generate revenue from the content they create. Google has a similar program, called Adsense. These programs allow you to share your content with the audience you have built. The news you present is watched very closely to ensure that you're not sharing hate speech, fake news, or anything that's been found to be inaccurate.

In February, I was approved for Facebook's monetization feature. The articles that I began sharing on my page were monetized with Facebooks ads. Businesses or companies that wish to have their ads seen on social media pay Facebook for a certain amount of views that their ads would receive. The monetization feature gave me the opportunity to generate revenue, which would then allow me to continue to grow my brand, expand my reach, and expand the team as necessary to grow. By March, my page had grown to over 300,000 followers, and my website was getting over one million visitors a month. Then, without any warning, without having received any violations, or even a notice of any violation, Facebook revoked the monetization off of my page. They even revoked the ability for me to monetize live videos that I was making in which ads could be inserted in the middle or at the end. Again, they did this without warning. Even though I sought for an explanation, they still have yet to give me one. I was simply told that it was revoked for 90 days, and I could issue an appeal after the 90 days was up.

It was a hard thing to handle. I was getting excited about the possibilities of where I saw the monetization could take me. It had been steadily increasing to over $100 a day, then over $200 a day, and then even over $300 a day. This revenue was opening my eyes to the possibilities of growing my own news network, focused on bringing the truth to the masses.

This was, I believe, a blatant attack and an attempt to control, manipulate, and dominate my voice on their platform. We've heard of other personalities that have experienced the same types of issues on social media platforms. Some friends of mine, in particular Candace Owens and Diamond and Silk, have had to deal with censorship and monetization issues. Mark Dice, who has over two and a half million subscribers on Youtube, got demonetized over his content. At one point, another friend, Jason Fyk, had over 25 million followers spread across several pages and groups on Facebook. In one day, Facebook unpublished most of his pages until he sold them to a rival competitor to which they felt aligned. He had to sell them for pennies on the dollar. This is why I decided to join a new social media company, one that's encrypted, and does not censor conservatives. They are not as big as Facebook yet, but I believe they have the potential to become even bigger than Facebook. For more information on how you can join me on this new social media platform, look for more information in the credits of this book.

Back to the examples of what I believe is at the heart of the new KKK. They desire to control, manipulate and dominate by any means available. So when you think about the fact that the majority of Americans now don't get their news from newspapers, but rather from social media and from news stations, understanding the importance of the capability to control the viewers with misinformation or distractions should make everyone understand what's truly at stake. So no, the new KKK isn't running around in the middle of the night with white hoods and gowns violently imposing their will on Black Americans. The new KKK is behind the scenes in high-level positions of authority and power that ultimately seek to do exactly same thing. While race was a driving factor for the original KKK, I believe control is the ultimate issue now, and control ultimately seeks domination. Race is no longer an issue, unless they can use race to divide and conquer us.

Our founding fathers created an amazing document called the Constitution of the United States. It grants each of us individual liberties, with the government having little to do with our everyday lives. This strongly opposes government having total domination and control. However, there is an alternative form of government that enables total control of the people. That form of government is called socialism. In socialism, the elites in the government control and dominate the people, literally dictating every facet of an individual's life. Venezuela is a prime example of a country that recently implemented socialism. They went from being a prosperous country with individual rights, to a country in which their people are in the streets, rummaging through garbage cans on a daily basis for food, even resorting to eating rotten meat when (or if) it's found. The only grocery stores with food are the grocery stores owned by the government. The prices of all the items in the grocery store are dictated by the government, and if stores seek to sell groceries at a rate different than the government has suggested, those businesses are prosecuted by the government. This form of government is a perfect mechanism to control, manipulate, and dominate the people.

It is truly a scary thing to think that our country has a political party (known as the Democrats) with a platform on which so many candidates are running for office on 100 percent purely socialist ideologies. The only way the government can offer free stuff is to take money from those that have, to give to those that do not have. The only way the government can continually provide anything for free is if they own everything. When they own everything, we, the American people, own nothing.

twelve

THE NEW CIVIL RIGHTS MOVEMENT

Before I talk about what I believe is the new civil rights movement that is upon all of us, let's take a look and be reminded of what the original civil rights movement was all about.

The original civil rights movement was a struggle for social justice that took place mainly during the 1950s and 1960s. The movement was for Blacks to gain equal rights under the law in the United States. While the Civil War had officially abolished slavery, it did not end discrimination against Blacks. Blacks continued to endure the disastrous effects of racism, especially in the Democratic South.

By the mid-1900s, Black Americans had had enough of the prejudice and violence that had been perpetrated against them. They, along with many whites, mobilized, and began an unprecedented fight for equality that lasted nearly 20 years. During the Reconstruction era, Blacks took on leadership roles like never before. They held public office, sought legislative changes for equality, and fought for the right to vote. I believe it's also important to know that there were 22 Black Americans in Congress by 1900 - and they were all Republicans! The

Democrats did not elect their first black individual to Congress until 1935.

In 1868, the 14th amendment to the Constitution gave Blacks equal protection under the law. The 14th Amendment was opposed by all Democrats. In 1870, the 15th Amendment granted Blacks the right to vote, and again, the 15th Amendment was opposed by all Democrats. Still, many whites, especially those in the South, were unhappy with the fact that the people they had once enslaved were now (more or less) on equal playing fields. To marginalize blacks and to keep them separate from whites, and to erase the progress that blacks had made during Reconstruction, Democrats implemented Jim Crow laws in the South. Blacks couldn't use the same public facilities as whites. Blacks couldn't live in many of the same towns, or even go to the same schools as whites. Interracial marriages were illegal, and most blacks couldn't vote because they were unable to pass voter literacy tests.

On December 1, 1955, a 42-year-old woman named Rosa Parks was on a bus on her way home from work. The segregation laws at the time stated the Blacks must sit in designated seats at the back of the bus, and Rosa had complied. When a white man got on the bus and couldn't find a seat in the white section at the front of the bus, the bus driver instructed Rosa Parks and three other Blacks to give up their seats. Rosa refused, and she was arrested. Word of her arrest ignited outrage and the support of the Black community. Rosa Parks unwittingly became the mother of the original civil rights movement. Dr. Martin Luther King Jr. took a role in the movement, and wound up front and center in the fight for civil rights.

While their fight was won, and civil rights slowly began to become a norm for Black Americans, today I believe there is a need for a new civil rights movement, a movement for Blacks to gain a sense of equality among other Blacks, and to take their rightful place in this country. Today, the majority of oppression, violence, and even the murder of Black Americans is not at the hands of white Americans or the KKK, but it is overwhelmingly (and sadly) at the hands of other Black Americans. In New York City, there are more black babies aborted in a year's time than are born. This is a self-induced genocide, and it has to STOP! We *have* to reverse it. I believe Blexit is part of the answer.

This past summer (2018), on behalf of Turning Point USA[93], I was invited by Brandon Tatum and Candace Owens to a Black Leadership retreat. The Founder of TPUSA, Charlie Kirk, is an incredible young man. He started TPUSA at just 19 years old, and TPUSA has now become one of the largest and most strategic organizations designed to support conservative awareness on campuses around the country, and is standing in the face of the very ideologies that seek to strip away our freedoms. Charlie was in attendance at the retreat as well. His skin is not black, but after getting to spend some time with him, he is, without a doubt, my brother from another mother…

At this event we listened to Charlie, Candace, and Brandon share their hearts and ideas of how they plan to wake up the black community. They were planning the first ever Young Black Leadership Summit aimed at sponsoring 300 youth from the Black community between the ages of 14-35, with the goal of bringing those youth of the Black community and covering all costs associated with the event. At the Summit, they will hear amazing speakers share their hearts and their hopes for America. I am one of those speakers this year. I am so excited!!! It is an open event to anyone that wants to join us.

Candace also shared her heart for reaching the Black community through a movement called Blexit (a term derived from the words Black and Exit). It's a movement aimed at reaching the Black community in the inner cities around the country, and supports the concept of free thought, choosing to think for ourselves, instead of our thoughts being dictated to us by our parents or our culture. After hearing Candace and Brandon share their vision for Blexit, they asked us each to record a video sharing our thoughts about it.

When I first heard Candace share her heart about the agenda of waking the Black community, and her dream to unloose them from the chains that have kept so many millions in mental bondage for decades, my spirit leapt. I was so excited to be a part of a movement aimed at helping to free the minds of my Black brothers and sisters in this country! You see, I believe that the first civil rights movement which Dr. Martin Luther King Jr. spearheaded, that movement for which Rosa Parks was a catalyst, was a movement to unite Black America, and blacks were inspired to rally behind the common goals of unity, love and freedom. It's only with unity and love can we as Black Americans truly see freedom. The New Civil Rights Movement, is to challenge Black America to wake up to the realities of how disconnected we have become. And identify what forces are seeking our ultimate destruction. It's a movement that calls out the greatness in each of us, and seeks to rid our communities of the oppressive behaviors that have created our demise.

As I was thinking about what to record in the video, my heart was gushing with words, ideas, and thoughts that I wanted to share. I prayed and pondered the direction for the video for weeks. When Brandon said to all of us that he needed our videos by the end of the week, I knew I had to get it done. I was praying and pondering - and then it hit me! I went straight in to my studio to record it. When I finished, it was about three and a half minutes long. I went to editing, and was able to edit it down to just over two minutes. The video you see on the Blexit website is that video. I sent it to Candace knowing that she had asked for videos to only be 60 seconds long, and even though I was hesitant, I felt that I had to at least let her see what I had created. She text me back and said, "oh my goodness. I love it, I freaking love it and it is going to be one of the premier videos on the Blexit website!

Chills, literally shivers, flooded through my body as I felt such excitement and appreciation. I felt that my Papa had given me a perspective to share in that video, and it resonated with Candace. In case you haven't been to Blexit.com yet, here's the transcript from that video…

MY BLEXIT VIDEO

"I am a part of something absolutely amazing and beautiful - the Black community. The Black community in this country shares a camaraderie and a bond where I can travel almost anywhere in the country and just seeing another Black American, I can get a head nod and give one to return that just says, "you're my brother... you're my sister".

That bond has been under attack.

I believe that we have allowed something to creep into the hearts and minds of Black Americans around this country that chooses to say,

"If you don't think the way I do, you are no longer my brother, you are no longer my sister".

That saddens me. It saddens me to think that Black Americans have allowed ourselves to divide ourselves and ostracize ourselves based on our beliefs.

I am a conservative. And I'm not a conservative because my mother or my father told me to be. I'm a conservative because of what conservative values stand for.

And I am so excited to see so many other Black Americans wake up to the revelation that they don't have to think the way their mothers, their fathers, their aunts, their uncles or their cousins all told them that they had to think. That they can choose to think for themselves.

I'm a part of Blexit, which is a family of Black Americans that choose to say, "I can think for myself, and I will love my Black brothers and sisters, regardless of what their political beliefs are".

Blexit is an awakening of the minds of Black Americans that I think, that I believe... will change the face of America forever.

It's a movement of love, and of understanding, and of thought.

It's a movement that says, "I can choose to think and believe how I want to, based on my own research... and I will choose to love my brothers and sisters, regardless."

I am so excited for what I see taking place in the hearts and minds of Black Americans around the country...

An awakening has started, and Blacks are exiting from the monolithic thought that has kept us in chains and bondage for far too long.

I am David J Harris Jr, and I am a part of Blexit."

Candace called me tonight to show me a preview of the Blexit website and to show me exactly where my video would be. I was blown away to see this massive movement that is aimed at encouraging the Black community to not to continue with business as usual in the way of politics (i.e. all Blacks voting Democrat blindly, regardless of the issues and topics), and that I was going to get to be a part of it.

I shared with Candace that I believe this movement that she's calling Blexit, is really the New Civil Rights Movement, and I could tell when she heard me say that, that she felt it. It *is* the new Civil Rights Movement, freeing the minds of Black Americans around the country from the idea that they have to blindly give their vote and pledge their allegiance to any political party. It's time for Black America to wake up, to do our own research, to rally together, and to seek to unite around the common goals and purposes that will help not only Black America, but will enhance America as a whole. Blexit is, The New Civil Rights Movement.

thirteen

A NEW AMERICA

I long for the day when people of all colors, backgrounds and genders can get along freely with one another. The Great Dr. Martin Luther King Jr. shared his dream of little white boys and girls playing together in harmony with little black boys and girls. He said "When the architects of our republic wrote the magnificent words of the Constitution and the Declaration of Independence, they were signing a promissory note to which every American was to fall heir. This note was a promise that all men, yes, black men as well as white men, would be guaranteed the unalienable rights of life, liberty, and the pursuit of happiness."[94]

Our society today is filled with so much culture that has been enriched by so many different individuals that there's no way anyone should ever be able to say that the shade of their skin gives them priority or a reason to be a victim.

Dr King said "But there is something that I must say to my people who stand on the warm threshold which leads into the palace of justice. In the process of gaining our rightful place we must not be guilty of wrongful deeds. Let us not seek to satisfy our thirst for freedom by

drinking from the cup of bitterness and hatred. We must forever conduct our struggle on the high plane of dignity and discipline. We must
not allow our creative protest to degenerate into physical violence.
Again, we must rise to the majestic heights of meeting physical force
with soul force."[95]

I think it's more necessary than ever for these words of his to ring
out far and wide.

I long for an America where justice reigns supreme, from the top
down, through our judicial system, our government structure, and
through all those that are in positions of authority over us.

I long for the day that those who hold such positions truly seek to
serve the interests of the American people and not seek to serve just
themselves.

I long for an America where our media actually tells the truth, and
reports the truth in such a way that continually seeks to inspire hope
for the future and not cause division.

I long for the day when our high schools and universities support
the notion of research to conclusion, and that they do not favor one
group over another.

I long for the day when freedom truly reigns supreme in the hearts
and minds of all Americans.

I long for the day when the Black community has completely shak-
en off the shackles of the past and embraced the opportunities of the
future.

I long for the day when those that believe as I do, that God is good,
and that He loves all mankind, are courageous enough to speak their
minds without worry of being ostracized in their careers.

I long for those days, but I do not believe those days will come on
their own. They will not just magically appear in front of our eyes.

Those days will become reality only when good people that see the truth, and that know the truth, speak the truth, and act courageously in the fight to bring this unity of love to pass. There's one thing I know for sure: there is evil in this world, and while there is evil in this world, evil men and women will plot and plan to carry out their exploits. In order for us to truly see days of peace, those days will come only because there is an innumerable throng of people championing the cause, and rallying the troops of love and righteousness to a far greater degree.

True freedom will ring when all of God's children stand in unity, one with another, side by side, regardless of race, color, or sex, and seek the source of love to move in them and through them out to the world. It is a fight that we are all in regardless of where you are, regardless of your age, and whether or not you feel like you have a voice. We are all in this fight. We all have an opportunity to use our voices, or to support those voices in whom we believe. We can all encourage others to listen to alternative sources of information to find the truth, and to encourage each other to research the facts and truly get a well-balanced perspective of what is taking place in our world.

True Freedom will ring when believers seek to love those that do not believe in the God of the Bible, not by bashing them over the head with scripture verses or telling them how wrong they are, but by loving them, by loving them the way that Jesus did. He *literally* laid his life down. He sacrificed him*self*. He endured unbelievable pain, torture, and drama in order to prove that He loved us.

This call is to those that believe. It's a call to pray more consistently than you may have ever prayed before - or to continue praying, but add an even greater desire and a fervor to those prayers. Add extra passion to those prayers to believe that God is listening and is counting on your prayers in order to enable Him take action. I do not believe that God is in control of everything. I *do* believe that He's in control of what we invite Him into. For some of you that may be a harsh suggestion (to say that God is not in control of everything). However, I will offer you the reasoning for why I believe this.

When we hear of something horrific that has taken place (say for example, a man has raped a little girl...), if we believe God was in control, then we believe that God made that happen. When we hear about a devastating fire that ripped through a town, such as what just happened in my hometown in Redding, California, and which wiped out over a thousand homes and took eight lives, to say that God was in control of that fire is to say that God caused that destruction and ended those lives.

If we say that God is in control of everything, when a mass murderer takes out over 50 people in Las Vegas (or whatever narrative you believe was the cause that ended those lives...), if God was in control, then we're saying God killed those people.

I ultimately look to God's son, Jesus. When he was in the garden the night before he was to be crucified. He prayed, "[Yet] I want your will to be done, not mine." He was yielding his will to his father's. He submitted his request to his father, asking him to enable him with the strength to carry out his mission. In the Lord's Prayer (the one in which Jesus said, "pray like this"), he says (speaking to Papa God)

"May your will be done on earth, as it is in Heaven."

In that one simple section of that prayer, he acknowledged that God's will is not always done on the earth, and that is why he tells us to pray "May your will be done on Earth, as it is in Heaven."

You see, I believe that in Heaven, His will is absolutely carried out. There is nothing that takes place in Heaven that's outside of His will. God is in complete control of Heaven, but he gave control of the earth to mankind. While there is an enemy that seeks to subvert God's will and our own with his will, we win when we choose to say, "Not my will, but your will be done." We are opening a pathway for God to move in and through our lives.

I believe true freedom will ring when people all around this country, and around the world, understand that when we seek God's will for our lives, we don't have to understand how it's going to take place, we don't have to see how things are going to unfold. But if we walk by faith, believing that God is who He says He is, and that he will cause all things to work together for our good; when we walk with that type of expectancy, then, and *only* then, is when I believe we'll walk in true freedom. THAT is when the world will finally hear Freedom ring!

SKYLER, JENNIFER, DAVID AND CORBIN

SOURCES AND CREDITS

1. "Obama 2016" - Dinesh D'Souza Movie

2. https://youtu.be/aUNc9bWu_1I

3. The History of NASA - https://www.history.com/this-day-in-history/nasa-created

4. Obama 2016 the Movie by Dinesh D'Souza

5. https://www.youtube.com/watch?v=IFqVNPwsLNo

6. https://www.youtube.com/watch?v=IFqVNPwsLNo

7. http://www.cjcj.org/news/8113

8. https://www.wsj.com/video/opinion-journal-missing-stimulus-money/62470847-A20B-4800-A6A1-84301FC9C13C.html

9. http://humanevents.com/2010/09/08/scandal-less-than-7-of-trilliondollar-stimulus-spent-on-infrastructure/

10. https://gop.com/the-real-obama-stimulus/

11. http://michellemalkin.com/2012/10/10/missing-in-action-stimulus-sheriff-joe-biden/

12. https://www.breitbart.com/big-government/2012/05/04/stimulus-money-a-slush-fund-for-unions-and-democrats/amp/

13. https://www.breitbart.com/california/2016/12/05/left-pretends-trump-inheriting-strong-economy/amp/

14. https://www.breitbart.com/big-government/2016/01/20/el-chapos-hideout-had-50-caliber-rifle-obtained-via-fast-and-furious/amp/

15. https://www.breitbart.com/texas/2015/12/15/five-years-later-family-of-slain-border-patrol-agent-brian-terry-still-seeks-justice/amp/

16. https://www.breitbart.com/texas/2016/10/11/wikileaks-gotten-press-clinton-asked-fast-furious-killing-ice-agent/amp/

17. https://www.breitbart.com/texas/2016/12/15/family-slain-border-patrol-agent-looks-forward-trump/amp/

18. http://humanevents.com/2011/10/04/fast-and-furious-bombshell-has-eric-holder-been-caught-lying-to-congress/

19. https://www.breitbart.com/big-journalism/2012/06/12/nbc-news-mentions-operation-fast-and-furious-for-first-time-ever/amp/

20. http://humanevents.com/2011/11/09/fast-and-furious-is-not-a-failed-operation/

21. http://dailycaller.com/2012/02/18/breitbart-on-why-the-media-tends-to-ignore-fast-and-furious-video/

22. https://www.breitbart.com/big-government/2016/01/19/federal-judge-rejects-obamas-executive-privilege-over-fast-and-furious-documents/amp/

23. https://www.breitbart.com/big-government/2016/09/09/office-inspector-general-report-atf-fast-furious-tactics-continue/amp/

24. https://www.breitbart.com/texas/2016/12/31/breaking-cartel-gunmen-fire-border-patrol-agent-arizona/amp/

25. https://www.politico.com/story/2012/06/holder-held-in-contempt-077988

26. https://www.breitbart.com/big-government/2016/10/14/more-than-1-million-lose-healthcare-insurance-2017-companies-flee-obamacare/amp/

27. https://www.breitbart.com/big-government/2015/11/20/revealed-democrats-knew-obamacare-co-ops-fail-video/amp/

28. https://www.breitbart.com/big-government/2015/06/25/supreme-court-upholds-obamacare-subsidies-6-3/amp/

29. http://humanevents.com/2013/08/15/obamas-unconstitutional-steps-worse-than-nixons/

30. https://galen.org/2016/changes-to-obamacare-so-far-3/

31. https://www.cnbc.com/2014/04/13/obamacare-launch-terribly-flawed-sebelius.html

32. https://www.breitbart.com/big-government/2014/09/26/busted-obamacare-website-cost-2-1-billion-twice-what-white-house-claimed/amp/

33. http://theweek.com/articles/464430/why-did-obama-adminis-

tration-spy-associated-press

34. https://www.breitbart.com/blog/2013/05/28/report-holder-felt-remorse-over-fnc-james-rosen-subpoena/amp/

35. https://www.powerlineblog.com/archives/2013/05/perjury-may-not-be-such-a-tough-rap-to-prove-in-the-eric-holders-case.php

36. https://www.breitbart.com/big-government/2016/08/10/fbi-irs-scandal-documents-obama-irs-waited-truth/amp/

37. http://www.foxnews.com/politics/2015/02/27/32000-emails-recovered-in-irs-targeting-probe.html

38. https://www.washingtonpost.com/news/federal-eye/wp/2014/09/08/irs-finds-more-key-hard-drive-crashes-claims-no-evidence-tampering/?noredirect=on&utm_term=.3df23ce26110

39. https://www.washingtonpost.com/news/federal-eye/wp/2014/09/08/irs-finds-more-key-hard-drive-crashes-claims-no-evidence-tampering/?noredirect=on&utm_term=.3df23ce26110

40. https://www.breitbart.com/big-government/2015/10/23/doj-no-criminal-charges-irss-lois-lerner/amp/

41. https://www.breitbart.com/big-government/2016/06/28/benghazi-committee-releases-final-report-slams-clinton/amp/

42. https://www.breitbart.com/2016-presidential-race/2016/10/20/clinton-campaign-obama-knew-hillarys-private-email/amp/

43. https://www.breitbart.com/big-government/2013/01/27/epa-

email-scandal-worse-than-originally-thought/amp/

44. https://www.breitbart.com/big-government/2013/04/26/new-york-times-reveals-obama-s-maneuvers-and-motives-on-pigford/amp/

45. https://www.breitbart.com/big-government/2016/12/22/house-snowden-report-says-he-damaged-national-security/amp/

46. https://www.breitbart.com/video/2016/05/30/former-ag-eric-holder-edward-snowden-performed-public-service/amp/

47. https://www.zerohedge.com/news/2015-12-29/latest-nsa-spying-scandal-world-learns-obama-lied-again-congress-furious-it-was-spie

48. https://www.nytimes.com/2014/03/22/business/fallout-from-snowden-hurting-bottom-line-of-tech-companies.html

49. http://articles.latimes.com/2013/oct/30/world/la-fg-nsa-diplo-fallout-20131031

50. https://www.breitbart.com/big-government/2015/03/25/white-house-silent-after-sgt-bowe-bergdahl-charged-with-treason/amp/

51. https://www.breitbart.com/national-security/2014/06/01/was-the-taliban-telling-the-truth-about-sgt-bergdahl/amp/

52. https://www.breitbart.com/national-security/2015/03/26/reality-check-six-soldiers-died-searching-for-bowe-bergdahl/amp/

53. https://www.breitbart.com/national-security/2016/05/09/obamas-foreign-policy-czar-knew-nothing-foreign-policy-really-good-lying/amp/

54. https://www.breitbart.com/national-security/2016/09/07/con-

firmed-obamas-entire-1-7-billion-tribute-iran-paid-cash/amp/

55. https://www.breitbart.com/big-government/2015/08/11/epa-causes-massive-hazardous-spill-in-west/amp/

56. https://www.breitbart.com/big-government/2015/08/17/epa-hiding-data-from-toxic-spill-it-caused-in-colorado/amp/

57. https://www.theatlantic.com/politics/archive/2012/04/gsa-threw-800000-party-and-all-you-got-was-bill/329797/

58. http://humanevents.com/2012/04/17/gsa-commissioner-neely-is-still-getting-paid/

59. https://www.breitbart.com/big-government/2016/09/30/gsa-report-concludes-obama-political-operatives-inter-fered-foia-requests/amp/

60. https://www.breitbart.com/big-government/2016/10/05/re-port-200-veterans-die-waiting-care-phoenix-va-build-new-back-log-cases/amp/

61. https://www.breitbart.com/texas/2016/03/19/texas-governor-and-senators-press-va-for-action-on-manipulation-of-veteran-wait-times/amp/

62. https://www.breitbart.com/big-government/2012/07/19/markay-on-venture-coporatism/amp/

63. https://www.breitbart.com/big-government/2012/04/14/mis-conduct-involved-significant-number-of-agents/amp/

64. https://www.washingtonpost.com/politics/white-house-fence-jumper-made-it-far-deeper-into-building-than-previously-known/2014/09/29/02efd53e-47ea-11e4-a046-120a8a855c-ca_story.html?utm_term=.48a753a8f3e2

65. https://www.cnn.com/2015/03/12/politics/secrect-service-scandals-gate-crasher-dui/

66. http://humanevents.com/2013/10/03/shutdown-theater-update/

67. https://www.stripes.com/news/wwii-veterans-storm-dc-memorial-closed-by-government-shutdown-1.244447

68. http://humanevents.com/2014/05/12/feds-release-more-illegal-alien-criminals-into-the-population/

69. http://www.metrolyrics.com/ultra-light-beam-lyrics-kanye-west.html

70. https://twitter.com/Rasmussen_Poll/status/1029749433129492480

71. https://www.breitbart.com/big-government/2018/06/01/trump-economy-black-unemployment-rate-hits-new-historic-low-for-may/

72. https://www.cato.org/publications/commentary/why-did-fdrs-new-deal-harm-blacks

73. https://www.bible.com/bible/111/1jn.4.16

74. https://www.babble.com/pregnancy/anatomy-fetus-placenta/

75. http://truthmagazine.com/archives/volume44/v440106010.htm

76. https://www.compellingtruth.org/Simon-of-Cyrene.html

77. https://dailycaller.com/2017/06/26/three-cnn-employees-resign-over-botched-trump-russia-story/

78. https://dailycaller.com/2017/07/06/cnn-is-still-pushing-the-

17-intel-agency-lie/

79. https://dailycaller.com/2017/07/09/the-media-perpetuated-a-clinton-lie-for-9-months-what-it-means-for-the-russia-narrative/

80. https://www.cnn.com/2017/05/04/health/pre-existing-condition-rape-domestic-violence-insurance/index.html

81. https://www.politifact.com/truth-o-meter/statements/2017/may/05/blog-posting/headlines-say-gop-bill-makes-sexual-assault-pre-ex/

82. https://www.washingtonpost.com/news/volokh-conspiracy/wp/2016/10/17/remember-its-illegal-to-possess-wikileaks-clinton-emails-but-its-different-for-the-media-says-cnns-chris-cuomo/?utm_term=.355ad2127b82

83. https://www.cnn.com/2017/09/05/politics/trump-doj-wiretap/index.html

84. https://www.npr.org/2018/07/30/633987811/trump-to-hold-news-conference-with-italian-prime-minister

85. https://twitchy.com/brettt-3136/2018/01/06/fake-news-cnns-brian-stelter-doesnt-recognize-his-own-words-of-caution-about-fire-and-fury-author/

86. http://www.foxnews.com/entertainment/2017/01/20/nancy-sinatra-slams-cnn-for-anti-trump-spin-on-story-about-her-humorous-tweet.html

87. https://www.cnn.com/2018/03/02/us/school-shootings-2018-list-trnd/index.html

88. https://www.youtube.com/watch?v=ha1ljAbOPnY

89. https://www.cnn.com/2015/03/05/politics/ferguson-report-

hands-up-michael-brown-darren-wilson/index.html

90. https://www.washingtonexaminer.com/cnn-scrubs-report-on-protester-calling for peace-she-called-for-violence

91. pic.twitter.com/ptxJmrbH9S

92. https://www.businessinsider.com/these-6-corporations-control-90-of-the-media-in-america-2012-6

93. https://www.tpusa.com/

94. https://www.archives.gov/files/press/exhibits/dream-speech.pdf

95. https://www.archives.gov/files/press/exhibits/dream-speech.pdf